3 9351 00

II0632258

ADVICE TO THE PLAYERS

───⌇───

Robert Lewis

INTRODUCTION BY HAROLD CLURMAN

THEATRE COMMUNICATIONS GROUP

NEW YORK

TCG gratefully acknowledges public funds from the National Endowment for the Arts, the New York State Council on the Arts and the New York City Department of Cultural Affairs, in addition to the generous support of the following foundations and corporations: Alcoa Foundation; Ameritech Foundation; ARCO Foundation; AT&T Foundation; Beatrice Foundation; Center for Arts Criticism; Citicorp/Citibank; Common Wealth Fund; Consolidated Edison Company of New York; Eleanor Naylor Dana Charitable Trust; Dayton Hudson Foundation; Exxon Corporation; Ford Foundation; Japan-United States Friendship Commission; Jerome Foundation; Andrew W. Mellon Foundation; Mobil Foundation; National Broadcasting Company; New York Community Trust; New York Times Company Foundation; Pew Charitable Trusts; Philip Morris Companies; Rockefeller Foundation; Scherman Foundation; Shell Oil Company Foundation; Shubert Foundation; Lila Wallace-Reader's Digest Fund; Xerox Foundation.

Advice to the Players was originally published by Harper & Row, Publishers.

Library of Congress Cataloging in Publication Data

Lewis, Robert
Advice to the Players
1. Acting. I. Title
PN2061.L39 1980 792'.028 79-3291
ISBN 1-55936-003-8

First TCG edition: October 1989
Second printing: December 1991

Contents

Preface

> Now that we've learned the notes, please forget
> them.
>
> —Pablo Casals

I was originally going to call this compilation of the performers' craft *You Can't Teach Acting*. Because, of course, you can't: no more than you can teach singing or dancing. If an aspiring actor or singer or dancer has the equipment and the talent, *then* you might help him or her to use themselves in the best possible way. A good teacher can give certain hints to release expressivity, or strengthen some technical weakness. That's about it. But then, those hints and that strengthening are indeed crucial for the performer. A good teacher cannot make an uninspired performer gifted, but a young performer makes a serious mistake in thinking that his natural talents exempt him from the need to study his craft.

The main danger in "lessons" is forgetting that work in the classroom (this book contains just a sample of exercises from actual tapes of my workshops) is only preparation for the stage, not an end in itself. Just as a scale you practice on the piano appears at some point in a Mozart sonata, or a step practiced at the barre turns up in *Giselle*, so, too, we must understand how our exercises, explanations, improvisations, and even discussions of the work of past masters are to be translated into actual rehearsal processes and into our perfor-

mances. I have seen too many "classroom" actors not to be
frightened of doing this book at all. The whole point is to
know that when you get in trouble with a role you can then
turn to your technical knowledge for help. Otherwise, forget
it. Martha Graham said, "The aim of techniques is to free the
spirit." Anyone caught on stage playing his technique instead
of the scene gives a bad name to any serious investigation of
the problems of the acting craft.

To help bridge the gap from the classroom to the stage,
it's a good idea to perform each *étude* with all the devotion
you'd (let's hope) give to a moment in performance. You
cannot do a simple exercise in class with poor concentration
and low energy and expect that by some miracle when you
get on stage as Othello the greatness of the part will infuse
you with a power and conviction you failed to cultivate in
your preparatory work. Not at all. A high "A" is a high "A"
—whether in the vocal studio or on the operatic stage.

Another danger of studying the acting craft is the tendency of teachers to separate the "inner" and the "outer"
work in the actors' instruments. There are thousands of man
hours spent in the training of voice, speech, and movement
while, elsewhere, someone is delving into our psyches,
dredging up our past emotional lives and organizing our
thoughts. This has led to two kinds of actors, those who play
classics or ponder problems of style but seem to be lacking
in some fundamental sense of truth to give those roles body,
and those who do not play more than five minutes away from
their own daily behavior patterns. If they do stray, they then
"bring the part to them," mangling whatever sense of form,
insofar as form relates to movement, speech, and a certain
"style" of behavior, the poor author might have expected.

So we have the meticulous performance of an actress in
The Way of the World who maintains faultless Restoration
posture throughout and whose impeccable diction renders
Congreve's *bon mots* intelligible (if not meaningful) to the

last row of the balcony. And yet she never shows us the inner life of her character, never reveals to us the psyche that we're asked to believe brings forth those marvelous epigrams. And we have the young actor, equally unsatisfying to the discerning theatregoer, who has agonized over every moment of Hamlet's emotional life, who has found meaning for himself in every last inscrutable word of this elusive role. But some of his moments are so private that no one beyond the second row is let in on the secret and he wears his doublet and hose as if they were his costume and not his clothes.

Therefore, in class, we must never settle for "what" we are doing and "why" we are doing it, but must also ask, "how" are we doing it? And, if we have found the "how," we musn't forget to justify it with the "what" and the "why." The modern acting talent ought to have a line from his head to his heart with the circuits ever remaining open and the line well travelled in both directions.

Now, about teachers stealing exercises from each other. Let me confess at the start: I have stolen and stolen, from my Group Theatre days to the present. And many's the time I've seen some spy sitting in the back row of my own workshop, surreptitiously writing in a little black book as some pearl is being dropped. "Please," I always say, "be my guest. How do you think *I* got it?" For it is not the exercises per se that matter, but how they're applied to a particular actor's need for use on the stage. Anyone can teach you the scales and arpeggios at the piano but not everyone is Rosina Lhevinne.

Exercises are not really "stolen" anyway—just "handed down." (You'll find one in this volume I lifted, in toto, from Joe Chaikin.) We all take, alter, update, add to, subtract from exercises passed on to us, some from way back. In *Method— or Madness?* I traced the lovely soprano voice of Marion Bell, whom I directed in *Brigadoon,* back to the Manuel Garcia (born in Seville, Spain, in 1775) method of singing. He taught his daughter, Pauline Viardot, his exercises. She, born in

Paris, taught Félia Litvinne, who came to France from St. Petersburg. Litvinne taught the method to Nina Koshetz, who was born in Kiev. When Koshetz took up coaching in America, she handed it down to my Marion Bell—and it still worked!

So grab what you can. It's all in the family.

Introduction

by Harold Clurman

There are theories of acting; there are no theoretical actors. "Artists," Andre Malraux has written, "Say what they would like to do, and do what they can." Every actor acts as his disposition and talent dictate. The playgoer reacts according to his taste and cultural formation. Actors and audiences of different nations vary in their appetites and needs, which enter into the formation of particular styles.

The "cold" acting of John Philip Kemble was very much admired in the England of the eighteenth century; in the early nineteenth century the "hot" (tempestuously emotional) acting of Edmund Kean became the rage. English acting today is on the whole different from what was generally the norm before the First World War. What is hailed as excellent in one era may be deemed false in another. Only our pleasure in acting remains constant.

Historically, the most famous theory of acting was set forth by Diderot in his *Paradox*. To put it bluntly, its thesis is that genuine emotion experienced during the actor's exercise of his art impedes esthetic truth and effectiveness. As Diderot developed this proposition it appears convincing— and is sound enough depending on what we meant by "genu-

ine emotion" *on stage*—but taken literally it is contradicted
by our observation as playgoers and the testimony of most
players. This is so if for no other reason than there is hardly
any such thing as wholly "technical" acting any more than
there is completely "emotional" acting, which strictly speaking would lead to insanity: Othello might really strangle Des-
demona! Acting at its best has at all times been crafted by a
balance of calculation and feeling.

A large library of dispute has been devoted to the matter. Teachers of acting wrangle furiously (sometimes insult-
ingly) over it. And while it may not entirely be a futile de-
bate, there is no exact ("scientific") solution. There are only
examples of acting we enjoy, deplore, or find indifferent.
They belong to every sort of "school," style, and tradition.
Rarely are they wholly of one kind; the product of one system
no matter what our personal preferences may be, all are
based on the demands of our own individual natures, our
artistic "metabolism."

What I particularly like about Robert Lewis' *Advice to
the Players* is that it eschews "theory." Any manual or text-
book on acting to be of value to the student cannot or should
not be "theoretical." Acting is a matter of doing, of behavior.
Only on stage or in active classes in preparation for the stage
can the novice become proficient in the craft. There is a
sense—and Robert Lewis is fully aware of this—in which all
books (except as criticism) pretending to instruct the begin-
ner in acting are, willy-nilly, fraudulent. At best they may
serve as reminders or guides for those who are already at
work in ongoing classes or productions. This is as true of
Stanislavsky's "classic" texts—*An Actor Prepares* et al—as of
all others. It is imperative to mention Stanislavsky here because the present book, like virtually all others in the contemporary (especially the American) theatrical "canon," is
derivative or sparked by that great Russian master.

There is no point in asking whether Lewis' book is "pro

method" or "anti method," "pro technique" or "pro emotion" (the terms are mere loose-lipped jargon), for to begin with the so-called Stanislavsky system—with him as well as with his heirs—has been and will continue to be an approach to acting in continuous evolution and never quite the same with any particular teacher or director. There is NO ONE RIGHT WAY.

More important still, the Stanislavsky system is a *technique*, not a dogma, a theory or a style—a technique variously practiced by actors in many parts of the world. (There were differences and divisions even within the confines of the original Moscow Art Theatre.) And the results are not to be judged by the success or failure of particular companies who claim Stanislavsky as their mentor.

There are, it is true, other techniques; for example, those of Brecht and Grotowski. But by and large most of these techniques relate to the Stanislavsky source. Grotowski has written, "I was brought up on Stanislavsky: His persistent study, his systematic renewal of the methods of observation, and his dialectical relationship to his own earlier work make him my personal ideal. Stanislavsky asked the key methodological questions."

Stanislavsky didn't "invent" his system. It is a formulation of what he concluded from studying the best actors of his time and the immediate past—none of whom had ever heard of him! Above all, it must be endlessly repeated, Stanislavsky, though himself a realist, never aimed at realistic acting exclusively. His teaching is relevant to acting of every kind: "Tragedy, comedy, history, pastoral, pastoral comedy. . . ."; in short, from opera to burlesque!

Lewis admits his eclecticism: He claims no priority in his choice of pedagogical devices. Together with comment, his book is chiefly composed of a series of exercises which he has tested over a long period with a host of students and which have produced unmistakably valuable results. He has chosen his "honey" from wherever he has found it good! He offers it to us in the same spirit. "Be my guest," he says.

The invitation is a clue to his frame of mind. His language is direct, familiar, canny and consistently humorous. His main characteristic is common sense, bred of many years as actor, director, and teacher in the theatre's many mansions. Contact with the stage in all its phases has taught him forbearance and modesty in view of the ideal, the practical, the institutional elements that constitute the living theatre as art and profession in our day and place.

ADVICE TO THE PLAYERS

Relaxation
and Energizing

Everything in the labor of art amounts to one thing: the difficult should become customary, the customary easy and the easy—beautiful.

—Constantin Stanislavsky

Place: The usual studio reserved for acting classes, i.e., a large airless room with several huge posts strategically placed to obscure vision. Windows that, when opened, let in the deafening roar of street traffic; when closed, result in mild but continuous suffocation.

Time: The middle of the night (10 A.M.).

Cast: Professional actors (and some whose résumés say they're professional)—about twenty in all—who believe acting is a craft, not an accident. Also, the teacher.

Props: Coffee containers and buttered bagels, wrapped in slippery waxed paper that the teacher is expected to retrieve from under the chairs after class.

EXERCISE:

Okay: everybody stand up. UP, up, up. Find a space where you won't knock into things. Medium base. This is broad base: ⅄

1

This is feet together: ⋏

And this is medium base: ⋏

Good. And normal posture: shoulders down, chest up, stomach in, buttocks under, and relax. Now, shake your hands. Hard, from the wrists out. Not the whole arm, just the wrist. Shake, shake. Hard, harder. You should feel your hands leaving your body. If you don't, you're not doing it, you're not doing it hard enough. Harder. Can you feel the sensation leaving your hands? Then you're doing it. Now reach for the ceiling and stretch. Up, up, up. Pull, pull. Up on your toes: ⋏ . Make a straight line from the tip of your fingers to your toes. If you feel yourself wobbling, just pull up. That will steady you. Higher, higher. Another quarter of an inch. . . . And slowly down. s—l—o—w—l—y down. Don't break. Now your fingers should be tingling. If they're not tingling, you didn't do it. All right, shake again. And sit.

EXERCISE:

Get yourself into a comfortable position in your chair. We're going, with our will, to concentrate on each section of our body and relax it if we find the slightest bit of tension. We're studying our muscles now.

From the right ankle down, concentrate on that right foot and relax it. If your toes, or any other part of it, are tense in any way, with your will relax them. Relax that right foot from the ankle down. Repeat this with the left foot, just from the ankle down. Now your right leg, from the knee to the ankle, that big muscle, I forget the name of it, relax that one. If there's the slightest bit of physical tension in it, relax it. Study it. Study your own muscles. You have to learn your own body. Repeat with the left leg. Get comfortable, so you can relax that whole muscle. Now the right leg muscle from the right knee to the pelvic region. That huge muscle in your upper right leg—relax that. Take any physical tension out of it. Now the left thigh muscle. Now both your legs should be completely relaxed. Check them over. If some little tension has come back into any section of either leg, relax it with your will.

Now the pelvic region, all those muscles in there, relax them. Okay, the big stomach muscles. Just let your whole stomach relax. Your whole chest now, relax. Now your right hand, from your wrist out. Relax all those fingers. There's a lot of tension in our fingers that we're unaware of. From the right elbow to the wrist, relax. Now from the shoulder to the elbow, relax that muscle. The whole right arm should be completely relaxed now. Repeat this with the entire left arm. Concentrate on each area, that's it, and study it. That way you will find out where your particular tension spots are.

Now relax your jaw. We have lots of tension in our jaws. Your cheek muscles. Good. And now the most vulnerable of all, your eyes and forehead. If you have any muscular tension there, relax it. See, your eyes aren't fluttering any more. Now your whole body should be completely relaxed; you're almost asleep. If you do this at home, and you should, do it lying down. It's much easier than in a chair.

Now, we're going to *tense* each muscle of each section of our body, one by one, and then relax it. We are studying the different feelings of tension and relaxation in each one of our muscles.

The right foot, from ankle to toes, tense just that area. I know it's hard because some of the other muscles want to follow it. But try to *isolate* just that area. Tense those toes . . . and relax. Now repeat on your left foot. Try to leave everything else relaxed. Next, try to tense your big thigh muscle, from your knee to your pelvic region, in your right leg. Leave the rest of the leg relaxed. Tense it and then relax. Repeat with your left thigh muscle. Now both legs again should be completely free of muscular tension. Now tense your pelvic region alone—not your stomach, not your legs—just that one region. And relax. Now just tense your stomach muscles. And relax. Check again that your whole body is relaxed.

Now tense your right shoulder only. And relax. Your left shoulder—and relax it. Your right hand, from your wrist down, leaving everything else relaxed, and relax. Your left hand. Tense your jaw, leaving your eyes and other facial muscles relaxed. And relax. Tense your eyes and relax.

Okay—everybody up—and *shake your hands.* Shake, shake, shake. Medium base, normal posture. Shake hard, hard, harder, and stretch up, up, all the way up, up to the top —and slowly down—and sit.

Now that we have done a few relaxation and energizing exercises, I'd like to say a few words about how these two elements relate to the craft of acting—otherwise you might think we do the exercises just to feel good.

Relaxation and energizing are the first two elements we explore in what will be a list tracing the craft of acting. All these elements add up to an instrument that is capable of transmitting to an audience what you are experiencing when you are acting: your feelings, your thinking, your sensitivity, your humor, etc. The first of these elements is a sense of truth. You'll understand as we go on that I mean theatrical truth, not personal comfort. Next is a sense of form. By that I mean inner and outer form, the subtext and the behavioral means to express it, plus the ability to choose and control those forms. Then there's the sense of style: the ability to adapt yourself to whatever particular means of expression a certain role, play, author, or period requires. Also, there is a sense of the *whole,* which is the understanding of the makeup of your part from the beginning to the end. Some people act well from moment to moment but lack this sense of the whole and therefore their performances don't add up, don't *develop* from the beginning to the middle to the end.

The next one, a sense of beauty. By that I don't mean prettiness. I mean that aptness of choice that, with its sense of form, enhances the mere truth of life and results in art. Take the cart in the Berliner Ensemble's production of *Mother Courage*, which rolled through years of war and was covered with dirt, grime, and blood. If Brecht, the director as well as author, were not an artist, he could have asked the prop man to splatter it with dirt, grime, and blood and it would have been a "real" cart. Being an artist, he had the wagon painted so that it *looked* as if it was covered with grime, dirt, and blood. It had the artist's contribution, a sense of awesome beauty, which is different from either prettiness or ugliness in life because it is something created. It is something envisioned, *chosen*. So it must be in acting too.

Finally, there is the sense of ease—that's what we're starting with—so that one does not notice the "workings" of the actor as he is acting. This is particularly important for the performing artist because we are looking at him as he is creating. Without this sense of ease you are in trouble. When you are relaxed, with no muscular tension, your technique is not apparent. Your emotion and your thinking can come through. If you are muscularly tense you will find that it is difficult for you to feel, or for your feeling to come out. It's even difficult to think. (Try lifting a very heavy object and doing a mathematical sum at the same time.) If you see a horrible accident in the street and you go into momentary shock, it's very difficult for you to cry or even speak. Your muscles are tensed up. After you relax, the emotion might flow as you try to describe the incident.

Stage relaxation is not death or sleep. It is that balance that is achieved between full energy and the feeling of ease. That's why I said to remember that tingling in your fingers. That sense of "aliveness" is stage energy. Stage energy is higher than life energy and, when it is coupled with physical relaxation, is the state you should be in when you are performing on the stage. Thus, the observer receives to the fullest degree the experiences of your instrument, inside and out. Michael Chekhov, the great actor and nephew of Anton, once said, "The highest point of our art is reached when we are burning inside and command complete outer ease at the same time." The reason I say stage energy is higher than life energy is simply this: the amount of energy needed to communicate, in words or thought, to a partner close by in life will probably be too little for the exact same scene to be communicated to an audience in a theatre, no matter what size. This is especially true in a "low-key" scene. In life, you might whisper so as not to wake the baby. In the theatre, enough energy has to be present to *transmit the idea* to the receiving public that you don't want to wake the baby.

Different actors are tense in different parts of their bodies. That's why we just studied our muscles, to find out which ones are tenser than others. When you find the places where you get tense, you must then do exercises that will relax those particular muscles. Some people, for example, have tense shoulders. Others have straight and stiff spines, as if they have ramrods up their backs. For some, hands can be a big problem. Watch actors' hands. Many of them are absolutely in knots. Yet other actors have tense jaws.

These particular tensions can distort your characterization, creating a block that stands between you and the part, adding something to your character that's not supposed to be there. Also you very often lose a part in auditions because a certain tension can make you seem as if you're not right for the part. If the character is supposed to be pure and innocent so that the audience won't believe he would chop his mother into little pieces as he does in the second act, the director will want someone who seems entirely ingenuous. If an actor comes in with certain tensions that are making guilty furrows around his eyes, the director will say, "Thank you very much," thinking that the minute that actor gets on stage the audience will know he's going to kill her in the second act. Happens all the time. Actors don't understand it. "He didn't even give me a reading," they say, baffled. There may have been some tension about your instrument that seemed to give you a whole *style,* a worrisome and distracting style for the character being cast. The best thing is to take care of these problems early on in your training. That's why it's the first thing we work on: so that you have a physical instrument that operates with a sense of ease, but is capable of tensing whenever you want it to and that *won't* tense when you don't want it to.

It's not a bad idea to do some of our relaxation and energizing exercises as a tune-up in your dressing room at half-hour. Let me also give you some helpful hints about relaxation *during* a performance. If you have a problem with muscular tension while acting, it will help you, whenever possible, to touch physical objects (in some justified way)—handling props, touching furniture, pieces of scenery. Your physical tension seems to go out of your body and "onto" the object. I often recommend this during rehearsals too. It's an especially valuable hint, if you can manage it, on your first entrance, where nerves can contribute to tension. I had a particularly long, nervous-making first entrance in Clifford Odets's *Paradise Lost.* I had to come in through an upstairs door, traipse all the way down a long staircase, and finally walk downstage to where Morris Carnovsky was waiting for me at a table. I worked it out so that my hand went from the door knob directly to the banister, down which I slid my hand till it got to the bottom. I then raced to the waiting chair at the table, grabbed that, and I was home free. From then on my talking and listening in the scene kept me concentrating enough for all tension to disappear.

You can also do little physical things during a scene to keep relaxed. In a love scene, for instance, you can touch your partner's hair, clothes, whatever. The tension goes off onto the other player just as when touching props. (I don't mean *he* gets *your* tension—I mean *you* lose it!)

I have seen actors working themselves up, physically, to come on in a big, explosively emotional entrance. Wrong. Whatever psychological preparation you may do (and we'll come to that later), you had best be completely relaxed *muscularly* if your on-stage scene is not to be tense and forced.

EXERCISE:

Let's try a variation on the relaxation exercise we did studying all our muscles. Get yourselves completely relaxed in your chairs. Check all your muscles. Now we're going to tighten a single muscle, leaving the rest of the body relaxed, and rise, walk around, and sit again in this condition. Ready? Tighten your right shoulder. Get up. Walk around. Don't let any other muscles get tight now. And sit. Relax everything. Now stiffen your whole left leg. Rise. Walk. Sit. Beginning to feel a bit of age, are you? A fresh student once asked me the physical sensations of old age since he had to play an ancient man. I said, "Simple. It's like slowly turning to stone." You'll be glad you have muscular awareness when you later have to play that up-tight military man or that laid-back rock star.

Body Work

When a man spends the least possible number of
movements over some definite action, that is *grace*.
—Anton Chekhov

EXERCISE:

Everybody up. Push all the chairs against the wall. Make one
large circle, facing in, all the way around the room. Now
check that you are equal distances from each other. Then all
turn right and face the back of the person in front of you.
Normal posture: shoulders down, chest up, stomach in, buttocks under—and relax. We are going to do some walking—
all kinds of walking, in different rhythms and accents. First,
walk in a circle with a 4/4 rhythm. I'll hit this little drum to
keep the beat, slow at first. Start on the right foot. Ready?
And 1—2—3—4—1—2—3—4. . . . Now faster. . . . Now slow
again (keep the circle wide). . . . Keep going and now I want
you to accent, with a stamp on the floor, a different beat in
each bar: first accent 1, then in the second bar 2, in the third
3, in the fourth 4, then immediately accent 1 again in the
following bar and continue the same pattern: and ONE, two
three four, one TWO, three four. . . . Now do these four
different accents in the *first* bar of each four-bar sequence
only and then accent nothing in the remaining three. . . . We
are now going to do the whole routine again, walking in
steady rhythm, accenting a different count in each bar, and

then accenting a different count in the first of every four-bar sequence—but this time we are going to walk in 3/4 rhythm, instead of 4/4. . . . And now the same thing in 5/4. . . . Rest a minute.

All right. Check your circle. We are now going to walk simply, in tempo (I'll keep the beat for you) and, as you start, begin to make your large circle smaller and smaller until you can't get any smaller. Then start slowly to open out till you are again as large a circle as the room will take. At this point start closing in again and keep repeating the pattern. Ready? Begin.

Okay. Halt. Believe it or not, we are now going to do the entire series of exercises *backwards.* Don't groan. It is important to enjoy developing this control over your body. Here we go, first walking in a large circle in simple 4/4 rhythm, backwards. And 1—2—3—4. . . .

EXERCISE:

We are going to continue our walking exercises with all the different accents. Only this time, instead of stamping your foot on the accent, I want you to limp on that foot. Let's start with the 4/4 beat and the accent on a different beat in each bar. First you limp on one, then on two, etc. We'll continue this through all the different accents and rhythms.

Now from the top again. This time, instead of limping on the accent, we're going to bend forward from the waist as far as we can. . . .

The next variation is to do the different walking exercises with our bodies held at various angles. For example, let's start the first simple 4/4 walk, no accent, with our bodies bent from the waist all the way to the left and our right hand over our head and to the left: . Everyone in position? (We do this with all the accents and in all the rhythms, occasionally changing the angle of the body: for instance, bent from the waist to the right, both hands over the head $\digamma$.)

Finally, we are going to walk with different accents and in different rhythms (as I call them out), but altering the shape of our circle $\bigcirc$, to a triangle $\triangle$, then a square $\square$, and finish with an oval $\oslash$. Ready? . . .

EXERCISE:

This energizing exercise is designed to loosen all your joints. Everybody stand up. Spread out so you have some space around you. Medium base. Hold both your arms straight out in front of you: $\dagger$. From your wrists out, make circles, right hand turning to the right, left to the left. Turn, turn, turn. . . . Now, from the shoulders, make huge circles. First the right arm, to the right. Go. . . . Hold it. Now the left arm to the left. . . . Both together. . . . And hold. Now, standing on your left foot alone, raise your right leg a bit off the floor and make circles to the right from your ankle down. . . . Now turn inward to the left. . . . Reverse. Right foot on the floor. From the ankle down, make circles to the left with your raised left foot. . . . Now to the right. Hold.

Standing on your left leg, raise your right knee high. Now make circles going outward with your right leg from the knee down. . . . Now circle inward. . . . Repeat with the left leg, standing on your right. . . . Okay. Hands on hips. Make large circles of your whole upper body, turning from the waist. First to the right. Turn, turn, turn. . . . Reverse. To the left . . . and hold. Now just your head. Roll your head in circles to the right . . . to the left. Hold. Dizzy? A small price for a good workout.

VARIATION:

Normal posture. Medium base. From your wrist out, with
your right hand, write your name in the air from left to right.
. . . Now write it with your left hand from right to left.
. . . Now both together, starting from the center and going out
to both sides. . . . Now write your name with huge letters
using your whole right arm from the shoulder . . . now the
left . . . now both together.

ANOTHER VARIATION:

This time we're going to write numbers from 1 to 9 in the air.
First, right hand, from the wrist . . . now left . . . both together.
. . . Now large numbers from the shoulder. Right arm . . . left
. . . both together. . . . Now, stand on your left foot and, from
the ankle down, write your numbers with your right foot.
. . . Now the left. . . . Now with your right leg from your right
knee . . . your left knee . . . now your waist. . . .

   That was so good, I'm going to give you a reward. Make
your numbers 1 to 9 with your pelvic region. . . .

EXERCISE:

Two volunteers, please. I want you to get on either side of
this table, lift it, carry it to the other side of the room, and set
it down. . . . Good. That's the basic movement. First variation:
do it with the absolute *minimum* of movement. Go. . . . Now
I'm going to tap out six slow bars of 4/4 time, twice. On the
second six bars, you go. Take the first two bars to lift the table,
the next two to cross the room, and the last two to set the
table down. Ready? And 1—2—3, etc. Don't lift the table on
the first three counts and then have five more to wait before
you start across the room on the second phrase. Take all eight

counts for each section, and land that table on the floor exactly on the last beat.

We'll try some more variations:

—Exactly the same exercise twice as fast

—The same exercise in 6/8 time

—The same exercise in 3/4 time

—Do the whole sequence again, from the top, but using an *imaginary* table this time

—We are now going to do the whole exercise with three people . . . then with four.

Lightness of movement, control of space, sense of rhythm, relation to the partner—all these are residuals of this exercise.

EXERCISE:

A good way to develop a sense of freedom, as well as trust, in your body is the game of Statues we used to play as kids. We'll do several variations on it. A couple of volunteers, please. Ralph, you take Rosemary by both her hands, swing her round and round, and then let go. Rosemary, you fall, completely relaxed, in whatever way you happen to land . . . good. Now, this time, end up in a predetermined pose. . . . Third variation: end up in the most beautiful pose. . . . And, finally, end up in the funniest pose.

Concentration

> If you have 100,000 francs' worth of skill, spend an-
> other five sous to buy more.
>
> —Edgar Degas

EXERCISE:

Everybody in the room has to concentrate during this exercise, because concentration, or the lack of it, is catching. If
someone on stage is not concentrating, it affects everybody.
Also, the audience doesn't watch the twelve people on stage
who are concentrating; they see the one person who isn't.
He's the one who stands out. That's why it has to be a com-
munal thing. So everybody participate throughout this exercise, not just when it is your turn.

We'll go around the room, starting with the first person
in the first row, and each person, clearly and with good energy, will say his first name to the next person. The next
person will take the name (or names), add his own to it, and
repeat the new list to the next person. If everyone is concentrating the class should get pretty far, with the list getting
longer and longer and no one forgetting. Don't mumble. Go!
("Joan." "Joan, Max." "Joan, Max, Dorothy," etc.) Good. We
got pretty far. Let's start again with the person we stopped
with.

When you repeat the name(s) for the next person, you
should not, as some of you are, be doing it for yourself alone,

14

but *for your partner* in the chair next to you. He, then, receives it clearly and, just as clearly, passes it on to *his* partner. Some actors forget this principle on stage too. They act for themselves. Let's not start that bad habit here. Let us use our sense of connection with our partners in our class work so that our exercises are, in truth, preparation for the stage. Give the names to the next person like a present. And it's also important in this exercise to try to maintain a regular rhythm. It helps you to remember.

Now let's do the same exercise but this time, instead of using your name, choose a single word—bread, cucumber, house—a good, simple word. Don't start with antidisestablishmentarianism. Remember, good energy and *concentrate*. Begin . . .

EXERCISE:

Everybody up. Now get yourself in a position where you have some space around you. Medium base. Normal posture: shoulders down, chest up, stomach in, buttocks under, and relax. Place both hands in front of your chest, palms down, middle fingers touching: ⊀ .

Now here's the movement: with a beat, fling both arms straight out in front of you. (Side view: ʈ .) Straight out— staccato, that's it—and back to the original position. Once more. Out—and back. But I want you to move out and back only when I tap on this table. Ready?

If you make a mistake and don't stop when I stop tapping, adjust at once. Don't call attention to your mistakes with little groans and giggles. Just fix it fast. If you're a wee bit flat on a note while playing your violin, you don't stop and apologize; you just slide quickly into place.

EXERCISE:

For the next exercise I need two people. Stand six feet apart, facing each other. I will give one of you a minute to observe the other completely. Then I will ask him to step in back of you and I will ask you to face the class and describe him and his apparel minutely, from top to bottom.

Notes after the exercise:

I'll tell you something about observation for an actor. Don't try to remember loads of detail the way one would memorize a column of figures. A lot of actors memorize their lines, their movements, their actions, and so on by remembering, "First I say this, then I do that, then I do this, then he says that, and so on." That's not the proper kind of memorization for an actor. An actor takes in sensations and gives out sensations, rather than totting up details like an accountant. If you have to study someone, as in this exercise, look at him with full concentration and get an *impression* of his whole being. Then take that impression and tell us in detail about it.

Concentrate hard: I'm going to talk now about concentration. The stage is full of obstacles dividing what should be your undivided attention to the work at hand. If you were a painter or a composer you could choose your time to work, when you were concentrating, and stop when you weren't. Performing artists, including actors, can't. At eight o'clock you have to get out there and work with your own minds, hearts, and bodies, your instruments of creation.

The biggest pull on your concentration is the audience. Even if the lights prevent you from seeing them, you know they're there. These days you see more audience than ever because so many theatres and productions are designed so that the audience are practically part of the play. Even if that were not so, the principle would remain. The fact that they are there watching you and judging you draws your concentration away from its rightful place.

The author's lines can be a disturbance to your natural concentration because they are not necessarily the way you would express yourself. Therefore, to be able to get that point over through someone else's means can be distracting. Your partner can be an enormous deterrent to good concentration. Not only might it be someone you don't like, it might be somebody who's not doing what you feel is required for the moment or is not looking at you when he should or is not right for the part or is not "giving you" what you need or God knows what else. Then, too, the scenery can be distracting, or the lights. Your costume may destroy the concentration you achieved so beautifully during the run-throughs without scenery and before you got the costume on. Even the props or your make-up may be a disturbance.

Most of all, personal problems may adversely affect your concentration. You may have had a fight with your spouse, a death in the family, or any other upsetting experience. Or you may hear a joke the minute before you have to go on to play a serious scene. All of these things make it difficult for you to concentrate. To divert the pull of these obstacles you must, with your will, be interested in some point of your choice.

In order to concentrate organically on what you want, you must be muscularly free. That's why we do relaxation and energizing exercises first. Conversely, muscular tension will tend to disappear if you are able to concentrate on the object of your choice. The two go together.

Concentration, for the actor, takes two forms. "Outer" concentration means the ability to look at someone or something that you have chosen and *actually see*. Actors often think they are concentrating on what they are seeing, but they're merely "looking" generally. Then, to be able to *listen to and really hear what you choose*—that, too, is outer concentration. When directors point out in rehearsal that an actor is not listening, the actor will often reply, "I heard what he said." But listening is not just hearing. You must listen with a dramatic purpose. To achieve these things you have to have strong, developed concentration.

Equally important is inner concentration. That means thinking of what you *decide* to think about and nothing else. You decide, as an actor, in this moment to think such-and-such, and with your concentration you are able to think that to the exclusion of all else. In life, our thinking can be random; but on stage, in order to point out where the drama is, you must be able to choose what you wish to think and eliminate those things that are not helpful.

There is also the control of the specific *circle* of concentration: to be able to concentrate on an area you have chosen and eliminate all else. For example, I could choose as my circle of concentration the whole world ("I don't give a damn what anyone thinks," I could yell) and send my message out to the entire universe. But I could take as my concentration point just all the people in this room. I can then narrow my circle down to those two actors in the third row. Mind you, when I am talking just to them it does not mean that I'm concentrating so hard on them that I obliterate everyone else. That would tend to make me tense. It's just that in choosing to concentrate on them, I perceive you other actors in the room a little vaguely. I know you are there, in my world. It's just that I am directing my speech to those two. But be careful of this tendency. You see some actors concentrating so hard you can tell just how much they paid for concentration lessons. They are making a fetish out of it, as they do out of so many elements of our craft. If you concentrate on your object, the rest will automatically fade out. It does not mean that the rest of the world is dead.

Finally, I can focus my attention on one person, right here in the front. I can even bring it down to this glass I have to drink out of. ("Isn't that a spot of dirt on the rim?") I can bring it down further to the tiny point on the end of this pencil. As in the shutter of a photographer's camera, I have now closed down the circle of my concentration from the entire world to the point of a pencil.

A lot of performers concentrate but they concentrate *generally,* on everything, so that we don't know where the drama is, so to speak. They fuzz up the scene. And what about those actors who stare into space a good deal of the time? In monologues especially you see it. They have not decided whether they're talking to their own mind, to the audience, to God, or what. You're the artist. You have to choose your object. It cannot be in some vague area, which is where a lot of acting too often is.

In real life, concentration is either voluntary or involuntary. We can compel ourselves to concentrate on something —reading a book, doing some task. Or our concentration can be pulled by something independent of our will. I try to talk to somebody but I hear a noise elsewhere and my concentration is drawn there. In a play, I would have to decide whether or not to allow that noise to pull my concentration away. On stage you can continue to talk over that noise or you can choose to stop, and so on. All is choice.

Now, how does all this work in rehearsing a part? The choice of the object of your concentration, the choice of the circle of your concentration, the choice of the amount of attention, all show what is important in a scene. Let's say my character notices that your lip is quivering. I might say, "Your lip is quivering," with my concentration on your lip. My action would be "to point out that you have a tic in your lip." But if I am playing a district attorney questioning you as a witness and I take the quivering lip to be a sign that you are lying, the focus of my concentration goes right past the lip, through your eyes and into your head. The action then is "to accuse you of being guilty." Even though the line is the same and the object, the shaky lip, is the same, by altering the place where the concentration lands, I've altered the drama. The drama in one case is about a twitching lip. The drama in the second case is about the guilt or innocence of a witness. That's why you have to be able to direct your attention to the exact place you have chosen. It is tied in to the drama. We do our concentration exercises not only because we want to improve our instrument, although that is of value as well, but because they help us in the actual playing of parts.

If, in a play, I come into a producer's office to get a part in his forthcoming production and the producer says, "Mr. Lewis, this is my secretary, Miss Smith," and I reply, cleverly enough, "How do you do, Miss Smith?" the kind of concentration (and the amount) I devote to the secretary in that moment will depend on my intention. If I just want to present myself as a nice guy to help me get a part from the producer, that's one thing. I greet Miss Smith pleasantly and get back to the producer to find out if there are any Chinese parts in his production since that's my specialty. BUT, suppose I feel Miss Smith, from the way she's looking at me, might help me to get in the show, put in a good word for me. I could use her. *Now* when I deliver my line, "How do you do, Miss Smith?" I telegraph to her that I like her very much, I'll see her in the outer office later, and so on. So, the degree and the kind of concentration I put on Miss Smith has not only changed because of my intention but has helped to change the intention. In this way is the element of concentration related to the *source* of drama.

EXERCISE:

Two people, please. Face each other, six feet apart. Normal posture. I'd like one of you to start to move any section of your body: hands, feet, head, whole body, anything, but do it *legato* and with a steady rhythm. I'd like the other person to copy his movement *exactly*—as if he were the mirror image of the first person. (This is the first of what will be many mirror exercises for concentration.) Whatever he does, do it right along with him, not after him. You have to concentrate very hard so that you can practically guess what he's going to do next. That's why I say *legato,* because if he made a sudden *staccato* movement, you'd naturally fall behind. Okay. You start, Joan, and Tom, you be the mirror image.

Notes after the exercise:

Joan, when he got a little behind, you went blithely on. As a result, he got further behind. That's wrong. You must *help* him to stay with you, using *your* concentration as he's using his and, perhaps, slowing down just a hair so that he can get re-synchronized. You don't just do your part on the stage and hope that the other person is going to take care of his part and, if he doesn't, it's his problem. It's not. It's your problem, too. The chances are *you* are going to look wrong too if the other actor does. The whole point is to *make it happen.* You should start with that kind of relation to your partner in exercises also. Think not only of making certain movements, but about practically *hypnotizing* your partner into doing them along with you.

EXERCISE:

Now let's make it a little harder. Two more people, please. This time, instead of keeping a steady rhythm, let the leader make his *legato* movement go faster and slower—in other words, with an *unsteady* rhythm. . . .

Good. Now let's try a variation: Do what we just did, the alternating fast and slow rhythms, except that, at a certain point, I'll call out: "Switch." Then, without a perceptible break, the person who was following becomes the leader and the leader now becomes the mirror image. After a while, I'll say: "Switch" again, and again you change parts. Understood? Go . . .

Now we come to a final variation. We'll do the same switching, only this time, at some point, I'll say: "No leader" —and we'll see what happens. By the way, keep eye contact no matter what your body movements are in these mirror exercises. If you turn your head all the way to the back, the mirror person loses you.

Notes after the exercise:

Just stand there a moment. After I said: "No leader," some movement continued until it finally ground to a halt. I'd like to ask the class who, during that time, seemed to be actually leading and who following? Sometimes one and sometimes the other? Do you two participants agree? Were you aware when you found yourself leading or following in spite of the command, "No leader"?

I'll tell you something about leading and following. In life, we're inclined to think of the leader—the person who initiates things, who starts conversations, etc.—as being a more forceful person and the one who is being led as the weaker person. It's not true in acting. There are some actors who are born leaders on stage. If you give ten actors an improvisation and tell them they're in a sinking boat, there's always one actor who immediately starts giving orders and becomes the automatic leader of the expedition. There will be somebody else who'll just sit there and worry about how to keep from drowning. As far as the scene goes, it does not mean that the person who takes the initiative is any "better." It's not a matter of moral judgment. The person sitting very quietly in that improvisation, wondering whether he's being punished for something that he did, may be giving an absolutely brilliant performance based on the circumstances of that scene in a sinking boat. He may be as "good" for the scene, or better, than the busy self-appointed "captain." In acting, therefore, you must not think of "leaders" as being *better* than "followers."

However, if you find that by nature, as an actor, you are a leader, one who "takes over" a scene, it obliges you, if you wish to be a complete artist, to train yourself to see the other side of the coin. As a "born leader," don't be so sure that you always know exactly what to do at once but try to find out what's going on, what might be some possible choices, and so on. Always be working on the other side of your personality so that you are not limited in the kinds of parts you can play, or to one aspect of a part. Conversely, if you are a natural "follower," you should train yourself, in these exercises and improvisations, to be more forceful wherever possible, to take the initiative. Incidentally, whether or not you're a leader as an actor doesn't necessarily depend on whether you are in real life. Acting is therapeutic for some people. If in life they're very shy, very often they're leaders of men when they get on stage. That may be why they become actors—not the best reason. You should be an artist because you have too much life in you to contain, not too little. However, it's your nature as a creator I'm discussing, not your nature as a person. Study yourself, discover the elements of your personality on stage, and work to fill out the weaker aspects.

EXERCISE:

Here's another mirror exercise. Give me two people. Face each other, six feet apart. This is called the "Director and Actor" exercise. First, the director makes four distinct moves and holds it there. Don't come back to the normal posture you start with or that will make it five moves. Just four. Use your hands, whole arms, legs, torso, head, whatever. Make the moves clear and rhythmic. Decide on them first and then go. The actor partner must then repeat the exact four moves immediately after. You can make it two measures of 4/4 time: the first four beats are the director's and, coming right in on time, the actor's four beats follow. The director must also concentrate on his movements so that he can repeat them himself. That trains your kinesthetic memory.

EXERCISE:

Let's divide the class into two groups. Group A, on a signal from me, is going to count, to themselves, in their heads, upwards by eights (8, 16, 24, etc.). Group B is going to try to distract them by calling out numbers at random (preferably *not* divisible by eight). You may get up and go over to them, but don't touch them. Just try to break their concentration vocally.

Notes after the exercise:

How far did you get? 320? Not bad. 250? That's not divisible by eight. I'll never know if your concentration was disturbed or if you're just lousy at math. Let me say a word to Group B. Some of you just made a brouhaha, calling out numbers and running around in a helter-skelter way. You created a general noise in which it's not too hard to concentrate, rather than picking out a victim, connecting with him, and trying to break his concentration specifically—for example, by repeating the same number over and over in his ear. This would drive him up the wall. In other words, you can concentrate quite easily reading *War and Peace* in the subway in spite of all the loud wheel noises, train whistles, etc., because that's all general noise. But if the person next to you says, quietly, "Hello," you'll react because that's specific.

EXERCISE:

This is a spinoff of the last exercise. This time Group A is going (on my down beat) to keep in your heads the words and tune of "Drink to me only with thine eyes," which is in 6/8 time and slow, while Group B is going to sing aloud the fast 4/4 tune, "Jingle Bells." Now let's rehearse to be sure we all know the words and music. First Group A. Now Group B. . . . Well, it's not the Robert Shaw Chorale but it'll do for an exercise. Let's go. Group A, retain your words and tune in your heads, keeping the same tempo we rehearsed. Group B, stay in your seats but try, with your loud and fast rendition, to disrupt their concentration.

EXERCISE:

Let's put two chairs facing each other, a couple of feet apart. Now, two volunteers. Peter, I want you to tell a story, either true or made up, to Herschell. Herschell is going to concentrate so hard that he is going to talk along with you, saying exactly the same words as you are saying, at the identical second. Impossible? Well, we'll see. You can do it if Herschell is concentrating hard enough to literally read Peter's thoughts and Peter is so determined to make Herschell echo his words at the very moment they're uttered. Once the story gets under way, of course, it's easier because you have the subject matter to guide you.

Notes after the exercise:

Try to give the partner a whole phrase, a thought, in other words, rather than a word at a time. It's easier to grab onto a thought than to guess what individual words might be coming next. Also, don't go too fast.

VARIATION:

Now we're going to do the same thing with two others. Tom, you start a story, Siobhan will say it right along with you and, when I call out: "Switch," without a break of any kind, Siobhan will continue the story, even if it's in the middle of a sentence or a word, and carry on as if it's her story. Tom will then be following Siobhan's version, just as she did his. I'll then say, "Switch," again and, once more, with no seam, the story will continue, wherever it is, with Tom leading, both saying the same thing simultaneously all the time. Then I'll call: "Switch," again, and so on.

EXERCISE:

Here are a couple of concentration exercises you can do at home. When you get into bed at night, if you've nothing better to do as you lie there before you go to sleep, go over your whole day in your head. But I mean your *whole* day, starting from the second you woke up. And I don't mean generally. Try to recall every detail of every second: waking up, looking at the clock, rolling over, getting out of bed, going to the bathroom, exactly what you had for breakfast, what you read in the *New York Times,* etc. If you do that— try to remember *minutely* what happened all through the day—you probably won't be able to get through the whole thing. You'll be asleep. You'll put Seconal out of business.

Doing this exercise every once in a while will help you to cultivate the most marvelous memory *and* concentration. But, more than that, you will have reconstructed a day in your life, instead of cancelling it out, as people often do. Artists want their experiences to remain with them because they never know what part of them they might be able to use some day.

Here's another one. Take a matchbox, a piece of paper, and a pencil. Study the matchbox cover for three minutes. Study it the way actors study, with your senses. Don't just list the characteristics in your head as an accountant would and try to memorize them. That serves to develop your mind, which is important but not everything. Look at the whole cover with such concentration that it's ingrained in your eye. Then put the matchbox to one side, take your pencil, and draw that cover. Get everything in—borders, size and shape of the words and letters, any decoration. When you're finished, place the matchbox next to your drawing and see how much you got—and what you left out.

It sounds like nothing, but it's a marvelous exercise. Not only does it help your concentration, but it incidentally gives you a little respect for a nothing object like a matchbox. That attitude will stand you in good stead your whole acting life. You'll never dismiss any object as being unworthy of your attention. Even a lowly matchbox can be a part of your craft and your work. You'll find, after a while, that instead of being wary of them, you'll love props because they're part of your material as an actor.

EXERCISE:

Here's a tough exercise that not only demands powerful concentration, but also drills your sense of coordination, as well
as group contact. Let me have eight people. Stretch out into
a line, all facing front. Now, starting from this end, tick off
the alphabet, the first person saying A, the second B, etc.
When you get to the eighth person, go back to the first person
to continue till you get to Z. There being twenty-six letters
in the alphabet, six of you will end up with three letters
apiece and the other two will have four. Go. . . . Do you all
remember your letters? All right, let's tick it off again. Concentrate, so you'll remember what your letters are. . . . I'm
going to read you a headline in the *New York Times.* Listen
carefully.

GOLD FUTURES ADVANCE; SOYBEAN PRICES ALSO UP.
Got it? I want you now to spell out that headline, the person
having the first letter calling it out (G, then the O, etc.). Start.
Please call out your letters with uniformly good energy.
. . . Now I'm going to set a beat and I want you to spell out
the sentence in rhythm. I'll set the beat with four taps on my
desk and then you start. . . . Okay. Now each time we fluff,
go back to the beginning at once and start again until we get
through the whole thing in perfect rhythm. . . .

All right, now the variations begin. I am going to give
you four movements to execute with each four beats. Also,
on the third beat of each bar, you are to call out your letter.
You'll want to accent the third beat because you're delivering
your letter then. But don't. Accent the *first* of the four beats.
Here are the four movements (start with normal posture,
hands at your sides): on 1, stamp your right foot; on 2, stamp
your left foot; on 3, step forward with your right foot, throw
your right hand straight out in front of you, and say your
letter; and on 4, return to position. Stop grumbling. This is
going to prepare you to *think in movement,* good training

for the inside/outside combination of performing we'll need when we get to all those parts where the character moves in prescribed ways different from your own. (And what about choral work?) Now, let's just rehearse the four movements by themselves. 1—2—3—4. Now let's tick off the alphabet with the movement, saying your letter on the third beat of each bar. Go. . . . I'll remind you of the headline from the *Times* again and we'll be ready to spell it out in 4/4 time: GOLD FUTURES ADVANCE; SOYBEAN PRICES ALSO UP. Ready. AND . . . It so happens that the first person has both G and O, the first two letters in the sentence. She's found out there's a built-in trap for her, which is this: the fourth beat returns the right foot to the original position and then she has to step out on the same foot again for her second letter. It feels funny because, as any dancer in the room will tell you, your tendency is to follow a right foot move with your left. Tough.

All right, thanks. Let me have eight others. We'll do a variation: I'm going to change not only the headline but the movement which, this time, will be:
1. Right foot stamp,
2. clap your hands,
3. left foot forward, left hand out, and say your letter,
4. return to position.

ANOTHER VARIATION:

The whole sequence with another headline, but this time in 6/8 rhythm and these movements:
1. Right foot stamp,
2. Left foot stamp,
3. Clap your hands,
4. Right foot forward, right hand out,
5. Hold the pose and say your letter,
6. Return to position.

Thank you. It's been a good workout and, if you're still speaking to me, I'll see you in class on Wednesday.

Imagination

Do not just invent something, but make something out of reality.

—Thomas Mann

EXERCISE:

I hold in my hand an ordinary pencil. Observe its properties. It is about seven inches long and it has a sharp point at one end. I am going to hand it to the first person in the first row. I want him to get up and, in a short improvised moment, use it as any object except what it actually is. Your little number can be with or without words. But be careful, since this is an imagination exercise, that your choice derives from, and is, some extension of this actual object and not something imposed on it with no theatrical logic. There's no point in taking the pencil, leaning down, and using it as a snow shovel, for example. Nothing in the shape or makeup of this poor pencil by any stretch of the imagination could suggest a snow shovel. But if I tap on my desk with it, raise it high, and give you a good down beat with it, it is believable that I am transforming the pencil into a conductor's baton. When you have finished your bit, hand it to the next person, and we'll go around the class. . . .

Notes after the exercise:

Don't turn exercises into charades. Don't get up and simply *illustrate* the idea that you are using it as an ear pick. *Do* it and do it well. I want to see the care with which you avoid injuring your ear with the object. Always seek the way to believe in what you do, whether it's a little exercise or a scene from a play. In fact, if you can't believe in your little moment in this exercise, chances are pretty good you'll never be able to summon the belief needed for your part in a play. One thing is sure: after these twenty or so different uses, we can never again have a strictly utilitarian view of a pencil. Our sense of the imaginative approach to props has been aroused.

EXERCISE:

Here's an exercise to drill your imaginative impulse. I am going to give the first person a word. Not a bland noun like bread, but a noun that has broad implications, like "religion" or "politics." He is going to leap up, without any preparation, and do at once whatever the word suggests to him. It does not have to define the word exactly. It need only be your immediate reaction to the word. It can consist of just a movement, or movements, with words or sounds or silent, anything—as long as it's brief and impulsive, not planned. When you've finished, you give the next person a word, and she will jump up, etc.

VARIATION:

This time we are going to give each other a famous name instead of a word. It can be a name from history, literature, contemporary or from the past—as long as it's a name that evokes an immediate recognition in everybody. Now remember, I don't want cliché charade-like *impersonations:* for the name "Garbo," I don't want to see you leap up and moan, with a Swedish accent, "I vant to be alone." Rather, do something that, to you, is the character's essence as it strikes you immediately on hearing the name. For example, the name "Goldwater" might propel you out of your seat into the character of a Cro-Magnon caveman. . . .

EXERCISE:

Ruth Draper, the great monologist, with the sole aid of a shawl, used to create women from distant lands as she imagined what their essence might be. This exercise is something like that. I am going to mention a country, anything from the United States to more remote places. I want you to take your time with this one, which is not concerned with your immediate impulse. Think first what the name of that country conjures up in your fantasy. Again, if it's Spain, don't just settle for a superficial impersonation of a Spanish dancer clicking heels and castanets. Try to arrive at some essence that is suggested by the name of the country. Then get up and improvise something that expresses that essence. Again, it can be silent or with words and, this time, you can make it a little longer.

I once saw Clifford Odets in a Strasberg class do "America" by creating a businessman waking up in the morning, realizing he is late, dressing frantically, gobbling down a quick breakfast, dashing out to his car, speeding to the office, dashing into the building elevator, running down the hall, plowing into his office, dropping into his chair, putting his feet up on his desk, and going back to sleep. . . .

EXERCISE:

We have done an exercise to develop your imaginative use of props. Now we are going to do one that will help you cultivate an imaginative approach to articles of costume. I have here a very nice torn sheet. I am going to hand it to Bill who, when he is finished with it, will pass it on to Mary, etc. I'd like each of you to create a character with this piece of cloth that will be recognizable to us all by the way in which you have used it. Let your imagination make a *distinctly* recognizable character. Don't just throw it around your shoulders like a cape and say: "I'm a woman." Use it in such a manner that we can all see at once that that's a burlesque stripper.

Imagination allows the actor to believe what might otherwise appear unbelievable. It helps you to create. It is, therefore, not something mystical, but a practical tool of your craft. That is why we work on these exercises—to develop our imagination. Otherwise, you become a "lowest common denominator" actor, simply presenting the author's words, the director's interpretation, the costumer's clothes, plus whatever personality you may have. The creative actor takes all these and, with his imagination, makes the part his own creation. That's the difference between an "Equity member" and an artist.

The use of the "image" in acting is the stage equivalent of "imagism" in poetry, in which you create/achieve/convey emotion not through concepts of things but through things themselves, which in art can only be realized through the image. An essayist can write an analysis of the institution of marriage, but Carl Sandburg simply said, "Wedlock is a padlock."

Our tools are not only words but thoughts, movements, costumes, props, make-up, and so on. Rather than taking a utilitarian view of his materials, the acting artist creates, with his imaginative point of view toward all these elements, something that is more than "just like life."

The artist sees beyond the facts, beyond what is there, beyond what others see, as in the analogy of the sculptor who walks along the road and sees a huge rock. Everyone else sees that rock and says, "Oh, what a big rock." The sculptor looks at the rock and something in its shape makes him say, "I can use that." Maybe he sees in it the figure of a seated old woman. He takes that rock to his studio and starts chipping away at it. Now everything he chips away is just as good rock as what is left. But it is unnecessary to the *vision* of what he sees in there. Eventually, by chipping away the inessentials, what is left is the statue of the seated old lady, or what he saw there in the first place.

There are a couple of gangs fighting in the street. A nonwriter, a nondirector, a nonactor, a civilian, in other words, says: "Oh, those rotten kids, fighting again." A playwright looks at the brawl and to him it can become a "battle for survival" or an "ego struggle" or whatever, right up to, and including, *Romeo and Juliet* and *West Side Story.*

There was an actor whose highly imaginative performances I tried never to miss during the thirties. (Actually, he is still performing.) His name, Joseph Buloff. Moments of his creations still stay with me, so illuminating were they. He made us see aspects of life in a new and different way. He once did a scene in which he was eating dinner at a table while having a Strindbergian fight with his wife of many years. I would not remember that scene if he had simply played it, like any competent actor, with intensity and character. It would have been a fight between a husband and wife in a play, the name of which I don't even remember. But I never forgot this scene because of Buloff's imaginative use of props. (Remember the first imagination exercise we did?) In the usual eating scene they give you mashed bananas or something else that is easy to eat and talk with. But Buloff wasn't an actor who wanted it easy. He asked for lettuce and salt and pepper shakers. He would chew on the lettuce and, on certain especially ugly expletives, the lettuce would fly out of his mouth like cannon fire. In his aggravation, he would violently salt and pepper his food, with one shaker in each hand, so that the table became a battlefield. One never forgot that there are certain kinds of marriages that are like wars.

In 1939 I directed William Saroyan's first play, *My Heart's in the Highlands.* In one scene, the old Shakespearean actor was playing his trumpet high on a balcony and the villagers, slowly drawn by the sound of the music, stood below and listened to him. That was the scene. It could have been just that. He could have played his tune on the trumpet and the people could have come around and really enjoyed it and gone off. I said to myself as a director, "Why are they drawn to this music in a worshipful way?" Because, I decided, people are *nourished* by art. So I fixed them all in a certain way so the whole group built up from the ground. Certain people knelt, others stood, some stood up on shoulders. I built them up like a tree. On top I put a tiny child held high. As the music played, each of the people took out of his pocket some gift he had brought, a colorful vegetable, a piece of fruit or bread, or whatever, and slowly offered it up. The tree seemed to be flowering as the music sprayed down over them. They all started to sway like branches in the wind. At the very end, on the last note, the little child held up a gaily colored chicken.

That was an example of the application of an image for the director. Let me now come to one of the great uses of a potent imagination in acting—for *justification.* You are constantly called upon in plays to justify certain things that you would not yourself normally do in that particular manner. Without imagination you cannot justify that required behavior, and that leads to the tiresome "I don't feel it" you get all the time. The actor should *welcome* unconventional demands on his thinking and his movements. The solutions, when found, inevitably lead to a more interesting performance.

A classic example of the imaginative use of justification was told us years ago by Maria Ouspenskaya, one of the early Russian theatre defectors, whose brains we were always eager to pick. Some of you may remember her vivid Hollywood parts—but all that was later, when, like some of her colleagues, she had to go west to pick up a few kopecks. Madame, as, of course, we called her, had a single scene in a play (if my memory isn't too fuzzy, it was with Walter Huston in *Dodsworth*) where she was on about ten minutes. She had worked her scene out very well. One day, at rehearsal, the director said to her, "Madame, your work is very truthful and very interesting but it's ten times too slow. It simply takes too long, given the relative import of the scene in the play. You have to go faster." She went home that night and, after momentarily contemplating suicide, sat down to decide what her choices were. If she was taking time in that scene, it was because she wanted to be sure all her points were conveyed clearly. She certainly didn't want to lose them. She could just go faster, but then she wouldn't be able to think or listen or get her ideas over. She also worried about her accent. If she spoke too fast, it would be difficult for people to understand her. What should she do?

She came up with three possible courses of action. First, she could go back to rehearsal and say she couldn't do it. You can always give up a role. She wasn't one to spoil a performance, which even the director had admitted was a good one. She dismissed that choice as being purely negative. Her second alternative was to do just what the director said and simply go faster. But then she would have to skip some of her points, she would not be able to listen as well, and she might not be well understood. By acquiescing to that idea she would have been as defeated as if she'd thrown in the towel. She vetoed that one, too. The third choice saved her.

She asked herself, "What can I do? How can I, in some way, *justify* what the director wants and not lose what I have? What would make me *seem* to be going faster without just rattling on?" The minute she asked herself that question, she came up with the answer. She had a taxi waiting downstairs. That's all. If you say to the cabbie, "Wait for me, I'll be out soon," and you have ten minutes of business to do inside, the mere fact that you know the taxi meter is ticking outside is enough to get your own motor going. She said she didn't even know whether she spoke faster or not when she next did the scene because she didn't think in those terms any more. She just knew there was a taxi there. On entering, she went directly to her chair *as* she studied his face, she took her gloves off *as* she talked. She was able to play all her points, her thinking was the same, but she seemed to get out of there sooner because she had to get back to that ticking taxi. The director was pleased and said the scene no longer seemed attenuated. By adjusting to a circumstance she gave herself, Ouspenskaya was able to *justify* what she was required to do. For that she needed to be an actress with imagination. Which she was.

As a director I have very often had to provide justification for actors, but it is part of *your* craft. I wanted an actor to sit in a certain position in *The Teahouse of the August Moon* while David Wayne, as Sakini, was translating the American lieutenant's speech to the villagers of Okinawa on a high platform upstage. The other actors were standing or sitting all over the stage. One actor was sitting on the lowest step downstage. I, as a director, wanted to have that actor arrange his feet and torso in a particular way that would make an arrow out of his body pointing up toward the speaker. The audience's eye would then go right to the main action even though the stage was filled with thirty or so actors. It is what Meyerhold would call "centering" the action. I asked the actor to position himself that way and he said he couldn't. I asked why not. He said, "It feels unnatural for me." "Who cares?" I answered. I told him nobody was paying money for him to feel natural. He asked why anyone would sit that way. "Think of something," I told him. "That's your job."

Well, he didn't think of anything, but he did it anyway, because he didn't want to lose his job, I suppose. But as the scene went on, he gradually sneaked his position back to the way he wanted to sit, i.e., comfortably. I called him over one day and said, "Listen. That thing I asked you to do embarrasses you, doesn't it?" He said yes. Now I had given all the villagers individual characterizations so they would not be simply a mob of extras. I asked him what his particular character did in the village. It turned out he was the local scribe. "Well," I told him, "don't you know that in the Orient scribes are all-round artists? They are also painters and dancers. They dance in the temple. They're total artists." I went on to explain that the position I wanted was perfectly natural for a dancer. I was making all this up, you understand, but he believed it and from then on he sat properly, in the position I'd requested, and he couldn't have been happier.

The point of the story is that that is *his* job. That is the actor's job. You don't say, "I'm not comfortable." Your comfort is beside the point. You're an artist. And, I may say, it is sometimes *agonizing* to be an artist. Of course it may be uncomfortable. But it's your job to say, "If that's what is required, in what way can I justify it, with my imagination, so that it now becomes theatrically truthful, even if, at first, it seemed to go against my sense of *personal* truth?" That's the purpose of working on these imagination exercises—to stretch your imagination. You should do them and do them until it is second nature for you to leap onto any idea, however awkward or unbelievable, and make it work.

To sum up, what you have to say to yourself is, "It is *as if* . . ." Those are the two little magic words, "as if." As a matter of fact, in our unashamed youth, we used to refer to it as the "Magic If." It is the springboard of your imagination. It helps you in that important need: the belief in what you do. It's the actor's faith. It also aids you to color, intensify, make fascinatingly true your inner actions. (We'll come to that specifically when we get to intention.) Olivier once said, "All acting is a lie." We can, with the use of our imagination, make it all *seem* true.

EXERCISE:

Volunteers for this one. Think of something that you can get up and do that will indicate to us exactly where you are. But I mean *exactly*. Don't just hang around, breathing, and then tell us you're in a park. Don't be general. It will be specific, for instance, if you are sitting in a chair, blindfolded, hands strapped to the arms of the chair and a huge bolt of electricity charges through your body. (You may also choose funny ones.)

VARIATION

Now I'd like you to volunteer to get up and do something that will let us know *exactly* what time it is. Don't just get out of bed and tell us it's morning. For example, if a certain actor in this class rushed into the room, slipped into the back row, and tried to look like he was there all the time, I'd know it was 10:15. . . .

EXERCISE:

Here's an imagination exercise that has that important resid-
ual: justification. As I said earlier, we have to use our imagination to justify what might otherwise appear senseless or uncomfortable.

I am going to assume an absolutely arbitrary pose. My
legs are slightly apart, my hips are thrown a bit to the right,
both my arms are raised, and my two hands are clasped to the
back of my head. Now I am going to study my muscles and
determine, with my imagination, where I might be and what
I might be doing. Okay. I am standing on a little platform at
one end of a room at the Art Students' League, posing for a
life class to earn some extra money. You notice that, as I am
saying that, without changing the pose, my body (the outside)
and my thinking (the inside) assume the truth of my invention. I can even sense the presence of all you art students
gazing at me and making marks on your drawing pads.

I have now justified what was merely a physical attitude
before. Very well. I am going to retain this exact position but
I am no longer in the Art Students' League. I am going to
study my muscles again and place myself in completely different circumstances.

Now I am at home in Irvington-on-Hudson and I am
looking out of my living room window at a passing sailboat
on the river. It is amazing how clearly the river conducts the
voices of the two people in the boat up the lawn to the house.
I am trying to figure out what they're saying. Notice how my
looking and listening (and thinking) differ now from my previous situation, even though my basic posture remains un-
changed. I am trying to justify this position in my present
circumstances.

One more. I am not in the Art Students' League and I am
not at home. I am trying to find still another reason for my

hands to be on my head in this way . . . Ah. I have been walking along Michigan Boulevard in Chicago when one of the kids of a group I just passed has thrown a small rock at my bald head—an irresistibly inviting target, I suppose. I have stopped and grabbed my head and I am trying to see if the impact has opened the skin.

You can use invented or real circumstances. My first two were fantasy, the last one, fact.

Okay—volunteers. Take a pose, and not one that appears to be decided beforehand. Throw yourself around a bit. Hold it! Now where are you and what are you doing? . . .

VARIATION:

This is a mind-boggling variation on what we just did. I am going to take not one, but four distinct and arbitrary poses:
—I squat down, torso erect, hands at my sides;
—I rise, throwing my right hand behind me and stepping back on my right foot;
—I step forward with my right foot in front of me now, my right hand extended in front, too;
—I return to normal posture.
First, I'll run through the movements once more to be sure I remember the sequence. (I am also studying my muscles to determine what I might be doing making those four movements.) Now I'll construct a logical story to justify this choreography as I repeat the movements:
—I squat down and pick up my fishing pole, which has been lying on the ground next to me;
—I step back and toss the pole in back of me to gain some leverage;
—I cast my pole out into the water; and
—I step back to await that huge bite I am bound to get.

You'll notice in this variation the poses may occasionally have to be altered ever so slightly to justify the invented business. But try to keep the original sequence as intact as possible. The idea is not to alter the movements to suit your story but, by studying your muscles, to create a story that justifies those movements.

A new scenario for those same movements: I am not fishing in the Hudson River. I am struggling with a mugger late at night on a New York street. He's just dropped his knife to the ground:

—I stoop down and grab the knife;
—I step back to keep him from getting it;
—I drive it into his belly; and
—I straighten up to see if I've killed him.

Now I am going to repeat the same four movements. Only this time I'd like a volunteer to tell *me* what I'm doing as I go into each pose. In other words, *you* create a logical scenario from the movements as you observe me doing them. I, on the other hand, will be sure to adjust my muscles, as well as my thinking, in order to justify the requirements of *your* imagination. This is all good training for that "total" (inside and outside) acting we all talk about and aspire to.

Now that I've gotten *my* exercise, it's your turn to design poses and justify them. . . .

5

Sensory Perception

In the studio you learn to conform—to submit yourself to the demands of your craft—so that you may
finally be free.

—Martha Graham

The subject of sensory perception and recall (also referred to
as sense memory) seems to have generated more nonsense
than any other aspect of the acting technique. It is one of
those tools that people have made into a fetish. I call it the
Hot and Cold School of Acting. You have an actor on stage
playing a man who's about to leave his wife, whose children
are dying, and whose uncle stole a million dollars from him
and now he's drinking a cup of coffee, trying to decide how
to proceed. As the actor plays him, all his troubles take second place to his reaction to the heat of the damn coffee. Or
else you might have an actor looking into an imaginary mirror, finding a speck on it, and doing a whole ballet about
removing that speck. Now, finding that speck is a perfectly
acceptable way of establishing the existence of that mirror
through sensory recall, but to parade your technique, as one
so often does in sensory reactions, makes a mockery of all
technique. Technique that is noticeable to the audience is
bad technique. Our purpose is not to exhibit our technique,
it's to play the play. It's not anybody's business how you
control your breath when you sing or how you sustain your

balance when you dance. Technique is not to be displayed but to serve you and the material.

To avoid the subject of sensory recall, however, and not do any work on it would be harmful because without well-developed sensory perception, there can be no truth in your acting. When actors have poor sensorial believability, their acting looks phony. They're showing you what acting should be, not believing in it themselves, not believing where they are, what they're touching, seeing, and so on.

An actor needs alive sensory reaction in order to make himself a vibrant instrument of transmission. The audience is the receptor. Actors are transmittors of all sort of things: thoughts, feelings, ideas, movements, looks, everything that makes up behavior. For all this to be clear and believable, we must have alive senses.

Also, the objects on the stage may be real—there may be liquid in the glass we are drinking from and there may be pictures hanging on the wall—but they are seldom the *actual* objects they are supposed to be. The stale ginger ale isn't fine champagne, the prop man's slapdash watercolor is not a Renoir. You are obliged, as an actor, to create, with your sensory reactions, the experience of drinking champagne or viewing a Renoir in order for the audience to accept the truth of those props. Mind you, they'll go along with you to a certain extent anyway if you "act" like you're drinking champagne. They come *prepared* to believe. But they do not get the genuine experience that is possible when something truthful has been created. It is the quality of their belief that we're talking about, not the fact of it.

Sometimes there are no objects at all, as in the case of that imaginary mirror I referred to before. I once directed a scene in which an actress had to look into a mirror that was represented only by a frame. She had to see the lines of old age appearing for the first time on her face. An actress could perfectly well look and see nothing and *indicate* that she was seeing something and the audience would have to accept it. But since the actress in this scene was Kim Stanley, a great deal more was accomplished. She was able to seem to be seeing, in actual detail, what was happening to her face and to react to it. The audience's experience was, therefore, richer and more memorable. They didn't only get the information, they *believed* what was happening to the character.

There have been instances of entire plays performed with imaginary props. Orson Welles produced an adaptation of *Moby Dick* called *Moby Dick Rehearsed* in which the actors had to pretend to be sitting in a whaling boat and holding onto the oars, feeling the sway of the waves, the sun on their faces, and so on. All the actors' senses were brought into play to create the decor and props. Orson knew that *Moby Dick* could not be done on stage with any attempt at creating the required realism but felt it could be performed in this highly suggestive, theatrical style. Naturally, the movements (harpooning the whale, etc.) required by the action, although *based* on sensory recall as we'll study it in a minute, were more properly recognized as "pantomime." Marcel Marceau's walking up an imaginary flight of stairs or capturing a butterfly, based on the sensory truth of those activities, is movement *evolved* from truthful sensory recall into descriptive movement that has aesthetic value in and of itself.

In addition to helping create scenic truth, there are further residuals if you have alive sensory perception. Moods, and yes, emotions can be enhanced by the use of sensory recall. To go back for a minute to that cup of hot coffee our fetishist friend made into the main point of the scene: if, for instance, you were having a fight with your wife over the breakfast table in a scene, your ability to experience the sensation of burning your tongue on the hot coffee at a crucial moment in the altercation could certainly *add* to your aggravation. A song of loneliness, sung on a porch in a musical I directed, was enhanced for the actress (and for the audience) by the addition of the shiver caused by the sensation of the cold night air.

One can sometimes use sense memory as a "substitution" in cases where you have no direct knowledge of the actual sensation desired. I mentioned in the First Lecture in *Method—or Madness?* how Jacob Ben-Ami, in Tolstoy's *The Living Corpse,* created the terror of blowing out his brains by recapturing the sensation of a freezing cold shower as he held the pistol to his temple. With the use of that all-important ingredient of imagination, one could, by truthfully sensing the agonizing pain of burning your fingers in hot fat, understand what the sensation of a burn over most of your body might feel like. Here, the believability is created not by the substitution of an analogous sensation plus a prop, as with Ben-Ami, but by a partial truth of sensory recall (the finger) plus imagination.

Even elements of characterization can be molded through the recreation of sensorial experiences. To arrive at an Oriental look the first time I was assigned the part of a Japanese man in a Group Theatre play, I studied whatever I could find on the physical characteristics of the Japanese people. (I later did the same for the Chinese as I got more and more Oriental roles, especially in films. I did so many, in fact, that many of my other cinematic nationalities began to look Oriental. I gave it all up one day when sitting at a preview performance of a movie in which I played a carefully delineated Nazi general, complete with Hitlerian moustache, Otto Preminger accent, and swastikaed uniform, I heard the woman next to me turn to her companion as I made my first appearance and say, "What's that Chinese man doing in that German uniform?")

I simulated a dynamic Japanese speech pattern, drew air in between compressed lips so as not to offend, blinked my eyes to create the reported visual weakness of Orientals, etc.

Then, one day, Sandy Meisner, a fellow Group actor, and I were out driving, the both of us crammed into the rumble seat of a car (*that* dates us). As I was talking to Sandy, the sun in my eyes caused me to blink and the wind in my face made my speech dynamic and my breath staccato. "That's your character!" exclaimed Sandy, pointing at my face. "What do you mean?" I asked. "All those elements you've been working for, one by one, to get your Oriental look, they're all there together right now," said Sandy. Thereafter, all I had to do before I started my scenes was to recreate the sensations of that wind and sun on my face and I was off.

Finally, I want to give an example of how, sometimes, one can arrive at all the major elements necessary for the playing of a role (inside *and* out) through sensory work. In Clifford Odets's *Paradise Lost* I played a weird little fire-bug whose business was setting fire to your factory so you could collect your insurance. My scene with Morris Carnovsky and Luther Adler, the two owners of the factory, was fraught with danger, as I had to simply *insinuate* my business proposition so that if it was unacceptable I could get out in a hurry. The combination of ingratiation and fear was what I was working for. One evening, during the rehearsal period, I was given an after-dinner drink of Cointreau. As I sipped the sweet liqueur, a malaise came over me that I seized on at once as usable for Mr. May, my part in the play. My lips pursed up from the sickly sweet sensation and, lo and behold! a tinge of fright went through my body, too. When I tried to analyze my strange reaction, I realized that what was making me slightly ill and upset was the taste and smell of the orange base in Cointreau. When I was a little kid and had my tonsils removed, ether was used as an anaesthetic. I remember my terror when an ether-drenched cone was clapped, with no warning, over my nose and mouth and I was ordered to breathe. Naturally, I held my breath to fight this awful smell (like dead orange peels). "Count," yelled the doctor, trying to get me to open my mouth. Bewildered and terrified (I thought they were murdering me), I kept all orifices locked up for as long as I could hold out. Forever after, that smell of stale orange peels was slightly traumatic for me. I even felt queasy once walking through the car of a train in Italy where the folks were all munching on glorious salami and bread and peeling dozens of oranges.

Now all I had to do was, just before my entrance in *Paradise Lost,* recreate the sensations resulting from the taste of Cointreau and my lips would purse up, a sickly, ingratiating smile would spread over my lips, and an apprehensive feeling infuse me. Naturally, when I came on with all of this going, I had *to play the points of my scene,* not carry my expression around, you understand. But I must say, as preperation for Mr. May, inside and outside, that sensory recall of Cointreau did the trick.

EXERCISE:

We'll do a few sense memory exercises in class, but you can always practice at home, too. The more you do, the more developed your sensory perception will be. The main thing to remember is that although they are *technique exercises,* they must be done meticulously. First, let's tackle the sense of touch. Here's my handkerchief—cotton, I believe. I place it on my table in front of me. Now, I'm going to lift it off the table, finger it carefully, then put it down again. All the time I'm going to study carefully the feel of the material, the slight weight of it, all its properties, concentrating hard so that I can remember the sensations completely. . . . All right, now that I've done that and placed it back on the table, I'm going to go through the exact same actions again, without the handkerchief, but recalling—no, *re-feeling—* the very same sensations. . . . Now, immediately, I'm going to repeat the whole thing *with* the handkerchief, in order to check whether I really experienced all the sensations when I worked with the imaginary handkerchief. . . . Well, I was pretty good, although I did leave out the slight feeling of warmth the material contained as I manipulated it. So, that's the procedure: (1) work with the real object, (2) reproduce the sensations without the object, and (3) check up on yourself, at once, with the actual object again.

You should do this exercise with all different materials —silk, velvet, corduroy, etc.

Next, go through the same routine with all sorts of objects—this ashtray, my pencil, a glass of water, etc.

Now you're ready to elaborate: take your hat off the peg, put it on, take it off, and return it to the peg. Always remember, after you have gone through the exercise *without* the object, to check back immediately that your sensory recall was complete.

Go on to even more elaborate touch exercises: count your loose change, sew on a button, put the kettle of water on for tea, and . . . well, you make them up.

We come next to the sense of sight. Take a picture (without too much detail, to start), study it with complete concentration—all these exercises have the bonus of helping your concentration as well—and, after a minute or so, put the picture face down. Now turn to a blank wall and re-see the picture on the wall. Immediately after, turn back to the picture and check up on yourself. What details did you leave out?

As a variation, you can study the scene outside a window. Then turn and see the same scene on the wall. Look back out the window to check. If you watch a jet plane crossing the sky, go back, after the plane has disappeared, to where you first picked it up and retrace the path with your sense memory. You'll have trouble checking up on this one, though.

Hearing: play a short piece of a record. Again, start with a simple one—maybe a piano solo or a single voice. Stop the phonograph and re-hear it. Then put the record back on and check up. Had you heard the surface noise? The mechanism of the tone arm? Elaborate now, with more complicated combinations of instruments, up to a symphony orchestra. Try both sad and lively music. You'll also find you are combining your sense of hearing with touch (putting the record on, snapping the switch, etc.).

A subtle sense memory exercise for hearing is this: with your fingernail, make a scratching sound on a surface. Now re-hear it. Then make the sound again and re-hear it in different locations—behind you, outside the door, etc.

By the time you come to the next sense, smell, you'll find yourself incorporating touch and sight. Work the same routine—the real object, then the imaginary object, then the checkup—with all sorts of perfumes and toilet waters. Then different spices and flowers, too, if you can find any around.

The final sense is taste, and this, of course, will include smell, touch, and sight. Work with all kinds of foods and liquids.

You will then be ready to devise your own combination exercises. Here are a few suggestions:

1. Mix a drink from scratch and taste it.
2. Make coffee or tea and drink it.
3. Comb your hair.
4. Put on your shoes and socks, not necessarily in that order.
5. Hang a picture on the wall.
6. Play your phonograph, after selecting a record from your collection and removing it from its sleeve.
7. Shave.
8. Find an art book on your shelves and open it to a picture.

It's a life's work, of course. But, even if you did only a few minutes occasionally, the rewards would be great.

We'll do some group exercises, too. For example, a tug-of-war. We'll take a long, strong rope and, with four fairly evenly matched contenders on each side, engage in a real tug-of-war. Then we'll drop the rope and repeat the whole experience with sense memory. You may laugh, but we're even going further than that. We'll add circumstances—a slippery floor or on the beach in the sand. Another variation will be that, in the middle of the tug, on a signal from me, the rope will break. *That's* a scrambler.

6

Intention

I trust in inspiration, which sometimes comes and
sometimes doesn't. But I don't sit back waiting for it.
I work *every day*.

—Alberto Moravia

Now for the big one: intention. Some call this element of the
craft "objective." Others refer to it as the "action" (inner
action, they mean, not physical action). Still others simply say
it's the subtext. The terminology doesn't matter as long as
you understand that this process, which is ever-present in
acting, is as important as breathing is in singing. Without it,
you turn blue. Acting becomes mere line reading and the
actor indicates what is supposed to be happening instead of
creating it.

This process is not, as some may think, a recent invention, starting with Stanislavsky and continuing with the
Group Theatre and the Actors Studio. To disabuse you of any
idea that it was "discovered" in Russia (or in America), let me
illustrate with stories of a couple of English actresses. The
late Edith Evans always asked to have her part typed out
with a blank space under her lines. In that space she wrote
what she called her "unspoken part." She put underneath
the lines what she meant by what she said—her thoughts
(intentions).

Mrs. Siddons, who lived from 1755 to 1831—way before

the "Method"—in her remarks on the character of Lady Macbeth, tells us how she arrived at a specifically worded intention in persuading Macbeth to murder. She studied the feminine imagery in Shakespeare's lines (never a bad place to look when deciding your intention): "I have given suck and know/How tender 'tis to love the babe that milks me," etc. Mrs. Siddons could have chosen the intention "to boast of (her) prowess." After all, the character does, in soliloquy, invoke the powers of Hell to unsex her and many actresses have played her this way. But, Mrs. Siddons writes, in the scenes with Macbeth, she used the tender imagery of maternal love and feminine virtues "to taunt her lord." Look to me, this tender, maternal woman says, and be ashamed of your weakness. And off Macbeth goes to commit his crime.

This example of a pre-Stanislavskian (pre-Victorian!) actress, working (before "psychology") in much the same way that we are discussing now, proves an artistic truism I've always suspected. It is not so much that some theoretician invents, or decides upon, a principle and then the artists absorb it into their craft. Rather, we study the great artists, try to understand what they do, and then set about formulating techniques to help us to those ends. After all, Stanislavsky, who felt himself to be a stiff actor in his young days, witnessed the Italian invasion of Russia by Duse and Salvini (Ristori had been there previously) at the end of the nineteenth century. He took one look at them and said to himself, "What are they doing that we are not?" One could probably trace the whole checkered world of the "Method" back to that moment. We know that Anton Chekhov, who was at the first night of Duse's *Antony and Cleopatra* in St. Petersburg, sat right down and wrote his sister Masha (March 16, 1891): "While I was watching Duse I realized why one is bored at the theatre in Russia."

So "Stanislavsky's" method (and here it is the *first* word we must rightfully put in quotes) is simply Stanislavsky's articulation and codification of techniques that working artists, not theoreticians, hit upon through instinct, experimentation, and trial and error.

Definition: Intention is what you are really *doing* on the stage at any given moment, regardless of what you are saying (or not saying, if it's a silent scene or if you are listening). When I say doing, of course, I mean doing *inside,* not whether you are smoking a cigarette or having a glass of champagne. It is, in fact, your reason for being on the stage. A line reading (and this is a term I dislike because it implies something like endlessly pre-prepared inflections) is not determined by the simple significance of the words alone, but by that plus what you are experiencing and doing at the moment. Your intention can be quite different from the obvious significance of the dialogue. It can be the same as the line's literal meaning, though not often, as we'll see, and it can be the direct opposite of the line. To illustrate: if I have to say, "I love you, Maureen," the way I say that is not only based on my understanding of the sense of those words, though that will always be included in the rendition one way or another, but by what I mean (intend to convey to Maureen) by those words. First, they could mean exactly what they say: that I, Bobby, love you, Maureen. (Intention: "to want her to know I love her.") You'd be surprised though how rarely, with good dramatists, this is the case. It's too foursquare. Such dialogue leaves little for the performers to contribute and it doesn't make use of the complex and unique medium, the live stage. You can stay home and read that play. Characters on stage who mean no more or less than they actually say, who imply nothing, are not much more interesting than their counterparts in life.

Second, those four words of dialogue could reflect any number of variations. For instance, I might not understand how Maureen could have thought I was in love with her just because I praised her acting in class. My intention now, with that line, is "to try to understand how she could have gotten that impression."

And finally, the words could convey the idea that I despise her. The author would probably put "sarcastically" or its equivalent in parentheses next to the line to make sure the intention "to despise her" is understood by the actor. It is wise for the actor to translate those "helpful" hints into intentions. That gives him something to *do,* rather than an attitude to mimic. Although, in the last case, I am letting Maureen know I despise her, I'm still happy to have the words "I love you," because the element of sarcasm colors and livens up the straightforward emotion of hatred.

I remember a joke we used to tell about Trotsky, which illustrates our point beautifully. It seems that Stalin received a cable from Trotsky reading, "You are right and I am wrong. You are the true interpreter of Marx and Lenin. Excuse me. Trotsky." Jubilant, Stalin read it to the Politburo. One of them piped up: "Just a minute, Comrade Stalin. Let me look at that cable. You forget, Comrade Trotsky is Jewish. Let me read it to you." Then, in a Talmudic, questioning singsong, he read it aloud: "You are right? and I am wrong? You are the true interpreter of Marx and Lenin? Excuse me! Trotsky." Here, by the alteration of the intention, we go quickly from "to confess my sins" to "to mock those *goyim.*"

I believe that intention is the most important element of the acting craft. In the studios of some orthodox "Method"-ists, a great deal of time is spent working on emotion. Affective memory is their big number. If you study with Stella Adler, the big number is apt to be "character." While it is true that feeling is an ingredient of performing and it is certainly true that you will often arrive at your intention through character work, I put the most emphasis on intention. More or less emotion on any given night affects the fullness and intensity of the performance, but this is simply a matter of degree. The *sense* of the play, however, is carried

forward through the intention, no matter how much emotional content is there to give it body. A wrong intention, or
the inability to act with intention, can distort an entire scene
or a whole play.

I directed a play once called *The Hidden River,* by Ruth
and Augustus Goetz, which was then produced in England
where I happened to see it again and was completely as-
tounded. The whole play had a different point because at one
moment in the first act an actor used a wrong intention. It
took place in postwar France and concerned an old intellectual who had been tried after the war as a war criminal
because he supposedly had collaborated with the Germans
during the Occupation. The action centered on his return
from prison and the reception he would get from his family
and friends. In the first scene a priest says, "I was present
when he was talking to the German general. I saw them
collaborating." The point was that the intellectual had been
talking to the German about Molière first editions, not the
locations of factories to bomb. They'd been students together
in Heidelberg. The priest has to make it clear that he means
the word "collaborating" sardonically. Otherwise there is no
play. The English actor delivered the line entirely straight,
as though they actually *had* been collaborating. Since the
character was a priest, you had to believe him. The play was
finished right there. The "high-minded" relatives and friends
treated the old boy rotten and they *should* have treated him
rotten. The actor's inner action should have been "to prove
the old man's innocence"; instead, it was "to prove his guilt"!

By the same token, an especially inspired and correct
intention can make history—not by distorting a play, but by
making us see the play in a startling new light. Eleanora Duse
was responsible for such a masterstroke when she played
Mrs. Alving in Ibsen's *Ghosts.* There is a moment at the end
of the first act when, through a half-open door, Mrs. Alving
sees her son embracing the maid and realizes that history is

repeating itself: her husband had been a philanderer; was, in fact, the father of the maid and had contracted a venereal disease. "Ghosts," she says, and, as most actresses play it, it sounds low, sibilant, and haunted. (I saw the Reinhardt production and it's even juicier in German—*"Gespenster!"*) Duse, in that moment, apparently made some movement with her fist indicating, through the choice of her intention, that instead of being overwhelmed by the past, as most actresses who play the role were, she would "fight off" or "free herself" from those ghosts. Here the actress nailed her interpretation of the play to the ground in one word.

I once directed a well-known actor (a highly respected and gifted actor, in fact) whose part called for him to make a farewell speech to a group of friends in the town he was leaving. There was a girl in the crowd for whom he had a special feeling. I asked him to look directly at her at one moment to bid her a special goodbye as he was making his speech to all those assembled. At that point I wanted him to play the intention "to give her a special goodbye."

"Where does it say that?" he asked me. "There's no line for that. The speech starts, 'Friends.' I'm talking to *all* of them." "I know you're talking to all of them," I answered. "I *want* you to talk to all of them. But just at that one moment it would be so nice to let her know you're going to miss her most of all. Do it as a favor to me—no one will even notice it!"

"Oh, well," he said, "if you want to rewrite—"

"Forget it," I said.

This actor was mysteriously unable to work with an intention that wasn't explicit, or even implicit, in his lines. But intentions aren't always right there in the lines. You must consider the situation and your relationships with the other characters. That farewell speech would have been enriched if the actor had added in this other small intention in that one moment—whether or not it had occurred to the playwright.

If you think that what I'm talking about has to do only

with the "realistic" form, you couldn't be more wrong. In verse plays, farce, absurdist plays, whatever, you need this skill all the more. There's no chance to make the dialogue clear if you don't understand performing in this way. The words themselves may exist in such an abstract or abstruse form that they *demand* the buttressing of intention for clarification.

Home, by David Storey, consists almost entirely of short, sometimes monosyllabic, exchanges between the characters. One might say, "The First World War," and the other would answer, "Yes!" I was sitting with Lillian Hellman at the New York premiere. She had spent her life writing well-made plays in which characters and situations were set up in the first act, developed in the second, and resolved in the third. Here, by the merest intimation, an audience was being held and moved. It hardly seemed fair.

But can you imagine what would have happened if John Gielgud and Ralph Richardson, who starred in the play, had been unable to express the inner life that was behind the words? Then, too, if you do a play by Harold Pinter where the stage directions, again and again, say, "Pause," or "Slight pause," or "Long pause," or "Silence," you can't just wait around in those pauses. Being an actor himself, Pinter expected that the players would understand that, in those pauses, however long they were indicated to be, they must either be continuing some inner action of the line before, or starting the action of the following line, or doing something entirely different from either one. But the inner life goes on, just as life goes on during the rests in music. The rests are part of the music. A rest is not nothingness. Intention is our inner music, and unless we are in command and control of it, we are in big trouble with certain new playwrighting or with difficult verse. In the "well-made play," the audience might be able to *guess,* even if the actor wasn't sure, what the character *should* be doing.

I saw an Off-off-Broadway play in the sixties the dialogue of which consisted entirely of song titles and their publishers. A typical line might have been, "Melancholy Baby, de Sylva, Brown and Henderson." (We used to do exercises like that but we never thought of charging money for them.) The characters included a young son and his parents—the usual generation gap business. After a family fight, the young man decided to leave home, but not before stopping at the door to say to his folks, "It's a Long Way to Tipperary." Well, everyone laughed. But they were laughing *at* the play, in a sense, and not with it. That song title could actually have been a meaningful line in that situation. I left home at an early age and it *is* a Long Way to Tipperary. The actor, however, delivered it as if it were just a song title. If the actors had imbued their dialogue with an interesting subtext, it might have been an interesting theatrical experiment. Since they didn't bring any meaning to the song titles, the play became merely a charade.

Here's a final, far-out example of the necessity for the continuous presence of intention in acting. Suppose I had to play the man in the moon. All I have to do is stand there, like this, perfectly still, feet apart, hands out to the sides, looking down at the earth. The thing that will change this from a piece of scenery to a character in the play is to give myself an intention. For instance, there's that young boy and girl down there lying near each other on the grass in Central Park. I am now going to exert all my moon powers "to force them to get together." You see, my position is the same, but where before only my body was used, now my whole being is flooded with this strong inner action.

Now we come to actual application. You always have to express your intention in terms of a verb. You want "to find out something from someone," "to demand something from someone," "to bawl someone out for something." These are all actions. I often suggest to people who have difficulty in enunciating their objectives to themselves to put the words "I wish" in front of their action. "I wish to understand why you're looking at me like that." It helps you onto the track of inner action and also forces you to connect with your partner or your object. You can't act nouns. A lot of people try to act "love" or "hate" or "impatience." These are all states of being. If you try to act them, you're just going to end up with some cliché of that emotion rather than one of the countless possibilities that exist within each one of those states of being. If it says in your part that you should say a line "with love" or "impatiently," just take it as a guide that the author intends that to be the *result* of what you do. But that's not what you do. It's simply an author's clue concerning something that may not be apparent in the dialogue itself. You, as an actor, have to translate that at once into an action that will result in that state of being. You may benefit by crossing out such stage directions. You may be tempted (I know I am) by such suggestions as "curling his lip," etc. Later, I'll show you how to write in your own actions that will give the author the result he wants.

Let's take "impatience" as an example. If you have to wait on the corner for someone who is late and you are impatient, the one thing you can't act is "impatience"—jiggling around, clenching and unclenching your fists, and so on. What you might do is (1) check your watch or a store clock nearby, (2) check someone coming far down the street who looks like your friend but turns out not to be, (3) take out your appointment book to be sure you have the day and time right, etc. etc. A person standing on the opposite side of the street (the audience, in effect) watching all this will think, "Good Lord, that guy's impatient." He, adding up all your actions, will know you're impatient. You, experiencing all those actions, will create in yourself the sense of impatience.

You must be sure you direct your intention toward some

object, whether concrete or abstract. You cannot just "console." You can console your wife or your child or yourself. That's why, to speak grammatically for a moment, we use transitive verbs (verbs that take objects) and do *not* use "to be" in stating intentions. "To be happy that . . . " or "to be sad" implies feeling rather than action and can lead to "acting" happy or sad.

Actions begin and end. They end by being finished or interrupted or they are interrupted and then resumed. My whole main action today is "to delineate the nature of intention." I will probably stick with that till the end of this session and that will be that. But suppose I suddenly notice some smoke coming in under the door. I stop for a moment, go to the door easily, so as not to alarm you, open the door, find out it's just someone smoking a pipe in the hall, and come back to my seat. I have interrupted my action, changed it to "to investigate a possible fire," and now have resumed my original intention. Of course, if it were a real fire I hope I would have evacuated you to the street, even at the cost of not resuming my original action.

In every play there is one overall objective, sometimes called the spine of the play. It is usually something quite general because it has to include the objectives of all the characters. But if it is a work of art, it has some unity to it. After you understand the play's spine, you are in a position to understand the overall action of your own part and to see how it derives from that of the play. Then there is a general intention going on in a scene and even smaller objectives within that. If a stage performance could be stopped and frozen for a second (the way they can do in film) and you realized that what you were seeing—inside and out—related to the whole fabric of the play, you could then say, proudly too, this is art, not life.

The way in which the smallest intentions derive from and relate to the whole play's overall action describes the inner life of the drama. When we see how the play's external expression—its structure, style of language, genre (comedy, tragedy, farce), setting, plot, etc.—meshes with this inside life, we're on our way to understanding theatrical form.

What you want to know now is: How do I choose my moment-to-moment intentions as I rehearse the part? After you have studied the material of the whole play, the first and best place to seek out your specific intentions is in the hints you get from the text itself. You know that particular "I love you" implies something other than its literal meaning by the insulting remark that precipitated the line, as well as by the door-slamming exit you make as you finish your speech.

The next big source to examine is the spine of the play. I'll improvise a possible rehearsal period of *Hamlet* as an example of the process of choosing intentions. Let's say that having read through the play and heard (in the director's production talk) that the theme is how corruption in high places leads to disintegration and tragedy in the society, I arrive at an overall objective for the play, something like this: "to try to survive in a corrupt society." (This is not necessarily the only or the definitive or even my interpretation of the play. It's simply a "given" for this illustration.) Next, you choose your overall action on the basis of the play's spine. Claudius's way to survive might be "to clear away all the obstacles to the throne." Rosencrantz and Guildenstern's "to serve their King," and so on. And Hamlet, in one way or another, might be attempting "to probe for the truth": the truth about his father's death, the truth of Ophelia's feelings for him, even the truth of life itself. So that in the scene with his former friends, Rosencrantz and Guildenstern, he might study their looks and behavior "to find out how much of what they're saying comes from their own minds and how much was put into their mouths by the King." We have now sifted down from the overall objective of the whole play to a moment in the action, thereby retaining a sense of theatrical logic in our choice of that last intention.

Another guide in choosing the specific way to put your intentions to yourself is the relationships between the characters. If you are irritated and say: "Please be quiet, I'm trying to work here," to someone on your level, a spouse or a friend, the intention would be different than if you are speaking to your child. In the first instance, the intention might be "to let her have it," and in the second, "to chastise her." The line hasn't changed and the wish hasn't changed but the color of it comes from your relationship to the other character.

The circumstances will also help you choose. There are two kinds of circumstances, those that are "given" before the play begins and those of the scene itself. The fact that Hamlet's father has died, suspiciously, and that his mother has quickly married her late husband's brother are given circumstances that will affect Hamlet's inner action in his first line in the play, "A little more than kin, and less than kind." The events that took place before the play began led to Hamlet's hostility toward Claudius. And the circumstances of this scene—a large, almost public, gathering—demand that Hamlet veils this hostility. In this case, as in many others, it is the actor's intentions that begin to clue the audience in on what the antecedent action is: another reason why well-chosen, and communicated, intentions are so vital.

Another source of insight into intention is what are known as character elements. Some characters lean toward strong actions, some toward sneaky actions, etc. If I were playing a straightforward character and had the line, "I don't want to answer that now," I would look the other character straight in the face and simply "refuse to reply." But if I were a sneaky character, my action might be "to skirt the subject." The way in which you state the intention to yourself not only derives from these character elements but these character elements simultaneously result from the specific choice of intention. Your particular statement of the intention puts you on the track of both your character and your feeling. Conversely, if you understand what your feeling and your character should be, then you are able to make inner choices that help you to those ends. For the purpose of explanation I am discussing these elements one by one, but obviously a character's personality, objectives, and feelings are so closely interwoven that you study them and explore them and discover them together. The inside and the outside develop *together* during the rehearsal process.

"Choice" is the operative word. How you choose your intentions and the specific way you put them to yourself determine what your performance will be and thus are significant measures of your artistry. If you have fascinatingly put intentions, your acting tends to be imaginative. If you have strongly worded intentions, the chances are that your feeling will be strong so that you're well on your way to the proper emotion.

One of the greatest stage actors I ever saw was Michael Chekhov, the playwright's nephew. In *The Deluge,* a sort of morality play, playing a businessman, he made a choice of intention so illuminating that I remember the moment clearly although I saw it in 1936. It was in Russian, but I gathered that the action took place in a disreputable bar full of crooks, pickpockets, and so on, all exhibiting the worst sides of their natures. At the end of the first act, someone runs in to say that the dam has broken and the waters will soon descend on the bar. They'll all be killed. During the second act, awaiting their doom, they all seem to soften up, repent. The second act curtain line informs them that the waters have been controlled and they are saved. The third act finds them all going back to their rotten selves. Something like that. It was in the second act that Chekhov pulled off his startling feat of acting. He was trying to explain to another businessman why he, Chekhov, had cheated him. It was the terrible circumstances of his life that caused his behavior, not that he hated the fellow or had anything against him. Quite the contrary, he had a genuine feeling of love for him. Now, had Chekhov only tried "to let him know he loved him," I wouldn't be remembering, or telling, this story decades later. What Chekhov did was to actually try, with a sort of digging motion, to get into his heart: in other words, "to become 'one' with him." With this psychological gesture he let us know the nature of love: to get inside someone, to become one with him. Not only was the acting of the scene memorable, but the artist, by his imaginative choice of intention, illuminated an aspect of human life for us. He found in this imaginary and contrived situation, playing a made-up character, the means to express a transcendent truth. That is how the acting artist operates.

For comedy, of course, the way in which you put the intentions to yourself is equally important. If you choose funny intentions, what you do is likely to be funny. You won't have to "act" funny or try to "be funny." You will have the *spirit* of fun. Funny bits of "business" spring from comically inventive intentions. I once played the suitor in Anton Chekhov's farce, *The Marriage Proposal.* The character was a mousey little man who was always fainting and I played him just that way—mousey. I had a little mustache of mouse whiskers and held my fingers together like little paws. Paula Strasberg played the landowner's daughter and she was completely yellow. She had yellow hair and a yellow face and we put her in a yellow dress. She looked like a huge Swiss cheese. So, instead of proposing to her, I chose "to nibble on her ear," "to sniff at her," and so on. The landowner father had a huge square beard. So, instead of begging for his daughter's hand, on certain lines I used "to swim into his beard," with my little paws. I didn't, in other words, have to "act a mouse." That's where we get in trouble when we work with comical ideas. We start acting the image instead of translating it into *action.*

You choose what you are doing depending on what you want the ultimate picture to be, but then you have to perform those choices. You can't pose for that picture.

Sometimes, in order to create an unusual color, you can substitute some inner action that seems quite the opposite of what a "normal" choice might be. For example, when I was very young I heard Mary Garden in the opera *Louise*. It was unforgettable. Years later I heard the opera again, performed by the New York City Opera Company. After the performance, my companion turned to me and said, "Didn't that girl sing 'Depuis le jour' beautifully?" (In the third act Louise, alone in a little house in Paris with her lover, Julien, sings of how life has changed for her now that, away from her oppressive work and her repressive small-town home life, she can breathe the free air of Paris, loving, and living with, Julien.) "Yes, beautifully," I moaned, my eyes filling with tears, "but you should have heard Mary Garden!" Someone passing by, seeing me, would probably have thought, "That man is describing something tragic." Actually, I was trying to describe something ineffably beautiful. For Garden had not only the ecstasy of love in her rendition, but pain, agony, all those indescribable emotions that are part of that ecstasy. In terms of my intention, then, instead of "to relish again something very beautiful," it was "to mourn the loss of the particular greatness that was Garden's." (Garden, in revealing the "other side" of ecstasy, was working just this way, so this anecdote serves as a double illustration.)

I am not talking now of the notorious "playing the opposite," which is often no more than perverseness. ("Playing the opposite" is when an actor makes a strange choice simply because it *is* strange.) I mean a quality I've noticed in great performers. The Spanish dancer, Argentina, had this gift. In her folk dance about a fishing girl she moved majestically. When she played a queen, she humanized her. In this way, she enriched all her characters. It's as if to say, "What's there is there. How can I look round the other side of it, not to change it, but to fill it out?"

People always ask, "What was so great about Laurette Taylor?" It's hard to explain because she was so simple, so devoid of mannerisms. Part of the explanation was this ability to include the other side. In *The Glass Menagerie*, Amanda has a scene with Laura on the fire escape and she asks her daughter to wish on the moon for happiness and good fortune. Since their chances for either were doubtful, Laurette realized that that was a poignant, sad line. So she tried to make a game out of it. That only made it sadder. On the other hand, when she was on the telephone trying to sell subscriptions to a magazine containing some cliché serial, she played it with all the frantic praise of someone who really believed in the story. She recounted it as if it were *War and Peace* because she needed the money from the subscriptions so badly. Laurette knew the speech was funny: she didn't have to make it funny. Strangely enough, or maybe not so strangely, the audience's awareness of Amanda's desperate life-or-death need to sell the magazines didn't make her fevered efforts to accomplish that any less funny—quite the contrary.

This process of choosing your intentions is where you, the actor, help to shape and define the source of the drama. One character wishes this or that—and that objective is received, accepted, rejected, whatever, by the partner, who has his own intention going, and this in turn creates a situation, a conflict. The choice of those wishes is the actors' moment by moment contribution to the play, to which the author has already made his contributions: the theme (e.g., good vs. evil), the metaphor (in situation and character), the structure, the language.

The actor must always "take sides"—even if you just enter an empty room and know that in a flash the bedroom door will open, your wife will come out, and you'll start the scene and tell her you're leaving her. In the moment that you stand there waiting for the door to open you must either (1) decide how you're going to tell her, (2) listen to hear if anyone is in there with her, (3) take a last look at this room you're never going to enter again, or whatever, ad infinitum. But you must *do* something, inside.

This inner line that supports the outer form—movement, style of speech, etc.—designed by the choice of intentions, interrupted, resumed, and so on, must be unbroken and fluid as emotion is.

Now we're going to do some exercises, silent improvisations for a single actor, to learn how to play with intention. We start without words so that we may first learn to control our *thinking*; we're forced to think about the intentions and not about the words.

For example, if I want "to prepare the class for the lesson," I could break that objective up into three small sections:

1. to greet you ("Good morning, everyone");
2. to call you to order ("Take your seats. And quiet please");
3. to check the attendance ("Henry, Janet, where's Max? Oh, there you are").

I can do the exact same scene silently:

1. I greet you with a smile, a nod, and a gesture;
2. I call you to order by waving you to your seats and tapping on my desk for quiet; and
3. I check the attendance by scanning your faces and marking off your names on my list.

In both cases, my thinking (the control of my main action divided into three sections) is identical. The only difference

is that in the first case I had dialogue and in the second case
I didn't.

EXERCISE:

For your first silent improvisation, the scene is your room.
You are an up-and-coming actor. The situation is this: You
come home and find a letter, which tells you to be (within the
next hour) at a certain theatre to audition for an important
director. It's a good part you've been hoping to be called for.

Your overall action in this scene is "to get that part." The
first section of that action is "to gather all the paraphernalia
you may need—pictures, résumés, etc." The second is "to go
over the audition material." And the third is "to get ready and
leave." Remember, the overall objective is what dictates how
you play the small activities. Since your overall action is "to
get that part," the pictures you choose would reflect that and
not be modeling photos, for example. Then, too, you don't
just check your lines (in your head: this is a silent improvisation), but prepare some way of auditioning that will get you
that part. Even "to get ready and leave," which might seem
to be a nondescript activity, must be motivated by your overall wish. To get ready to go to the movies or a swimming pool
or a funeral are all different from getting ready to leave "to
get that part." (I am explaining much too much, you understand, but that's only because this is our first intention improvisation. After this, you're on your own.)

In setting up your scene, do not place your props in
obviously convenient places. Create obstacles that you must
overcome. That makes for more interesting acting. (I never
can find that one particular photograph I'm looking for.)
Most acting consists of overcoming obstacles. One of the
things that used to be terrible about Hollywood acting when
I was there in the forties was that they never allowed the
actors any obstacles. They fixed everything for your comfort.

If you had to get up from a chair, they made sure the chair was far enough from the desk that it wouldn't need to be pushed back a bit and, horrors! maybe squeak a little. They removed all signs of life from the scene. Your acting, as a result, became absolutely antiseptic. That's why so many of the actors had those vacuous looks.

You must do the opposite. Life is not that well made and certainly stage life isn't. Letters aren't all that easily found and opened up. Create obstacles for yourself, but create ones that are in the nature of the problem you have to solve and that will make the solving of the problem more interesting and imaginative. Develop your sense of scenic truth so the arrangement of objects on stage is usable for your actions.

One final point. Remember what I said about the *flow* of inner actions. Although I gave you the three subsidiary activities carefully, it doesn't mean that you have to be four-square about it, to finish one completely before you start the next. If it is true that you have very little time before your appointment with the director, you might well start to think about the audition material before you find all your pictures and might start to get ready to leave before you finish going over the material, and so on. There is a natural overlapping and flow. Even in music, where the phrases are laid out with more regularity, a good musician knows how to blend, or break up, phrases to give interest to the form.

EXERCISE:

Here's another silent improvisation for one person. Your overall inner action is "to bid goodbye to a loved one." This is broken up into three small activities: to write a note, to tidy up the room, to find a photo. . . .

Notes after the Exercise:

Let's examine what you did, Helen. Was the person real to you? I don't care whether it was an actual person in your life or someone in your imagination. The point is was he specific as far as details of his appearance, manner, etc., go? Without that, a sense of truth is hard for you to create. Now, let's check the circumstances. What happened to bring you to this point of farewell? . . . I see. That seems a little vague and general. Now, about the room itself and the props in it—what we call our sense of scenic truth. It's important because it's hard to believe in your situation if you can't even believe where you are. And THE BELIEF IN WHAT YOU DO is the ground pedal of all acting. Now, was it your room? His? Both of yours? What references do you have for all the physical properties of the place?

Let's break your scene down into its sections and examine them. You wrote a note in order to say goodbye to this loved one. Can you tell us what you said in that note? . . . He could go and do *what* to himself? Well, that, at least, is quite specific. I hope I didn't embarrass you with the question. That's one of the occupational hazards of our profession anyway, so it's just as well you get used to it now. The tidying up seemed no different than if you were just getting ready for company. I didn't see what specifically the tidying up had to do with such a bitter farewell as you wrote. If, for example, he was the compulsive neatener you implied in your note, you could (mind you, this is just my suggestion—there are a thousand possibilities) have left everything just a little askew so as to infuriate him when he returned. Then the "tidying up" would be related to the "saying goodbye." Likewise with the photo. Did you *see* the photo, really? What associations did it have for you? You simply *found* it when tidying up, but I didn't see what you wanted to *do* with it as part of your farewell.

EXERCISE:

Here's one of the best silent improvisations for a single actor. It has almost everything in it.

The given circumstances are these: You have been walking down Fifth Avenue in New York City. Suddenly a strange-looking man comes up to you, gives you an envelope, says, "Don't open this until you're alone," and disappears in the passing crowd. You find yourself standing in front of St. Patrick's Cathedral. You go up the steps, pull open the door, and enter the Cathedral. This is where the actual improvisation begins. Your overall objective is "to find out what it's all about."

We'll divide that intention into our usual three small activities. (There is no "rule of three" in breaking down your objectives in a part. It's just a nice small number to keep improvisations from dragging on forever.) First—"to make sure you're unwatched." Second—"to open the envelope and read." Third—"to hear the door behind you opening slowly." . . .

Notes after the exercise:

Let's ask you some questions, Sam. First, we must check the truth of the circumstances—your belief in them. Exactly what was the man like? Did he seem genuinely menacing? That would lead you on to one set of choices. Did he look as if he just might be a harmless jokester? That would color the impression quite differently. And what did you think *might* be in the envelope? *It is not only important to know your given circumstances, but for them to be specific enough to you to affect your scene when it starts.* Now, about your sense of scenic truth as you entered the Cathedral . . . whether you are religious or not, there is a certain adjustment one has to an edifice as imposing as a cathedral. Don't just accept this studio as St. Patrick's Cathedral and have everything fall into place as you need it. I don't expect you to build a set here, but you should prepare your acting space before you start. Know where the door in question is exactly, where the holy water is, place the pews you'll need in the set up, etc. *Then* start.

Now take your first section, "to make sure you're unwatched." You, obviously a Catholic, performed your automatic rituals at once. What I didn't see was the presence in your mind of the thinking connected with "making sure you're unwatched" as you crossed yourself. Even if you are religious, the process of intention goes on from your entrance to your exit. It's true you looked around, but, miraculously, no one was there to disturb you. No one praying, no one resting, no sexton walking by. Not even someone lighting a candle, much less a baptism over in the far corner? What I'm suggesting is that if you take the easy way out, you do not complicate your problem with any obstacles that would make the solution interesting for you as well as for us. You might have had to move to another spot, for example. Or pretend to be praying and conceal the note in an opened prayer book to read it.

Now what did the note say? . . . Well, there too, that's a sort of lowest common denominator, the usual vague general threat on your life. Like a crime show on television. Why assume it has to be something cliché when you have the whole world of your imagination to work with, even something as silly as "Come and have your fortune told at the Gypsy Tea Room"?

Finally, when the door opened slowly, you chose it to be just another parishioner so you could simply get up and walk out. Actually, if it *was* just an ad for a tea room, the opening door might very well just disclose another parishioner. But you chose a threat on your life. Your invention ought, there-

fore, to lead you, in your last section, to choose something
related to your circumstances. Otherwise your choice, although possible, was dull.

EXERCISE:

Now I'm going to suggest a situation, but this time I'm going
to let you lay out your own subtext plan instead of my giving
it to you. I'm simply going to tell you that you come home
and, by some means that you will devise, you find news—
either good, such as winning a huge lottery, or bad, such as
learning of a death, or whatever. Make it important, not
trivial. What you do then I leave to you. This can be silent
or you can use the telephone if you wish. . . . (Exercises in
improvisation continue in next chapter.)

7

Improvisation

> In every branch of art—the work of preparation
> ruled by discipline should finally disappear, so that
> the elegance and freshness of the form should strike
> us as being spontaneous.
>
> —Pablo Casals

Improvisation, first of all, has been a style of theatre all the way from the *commedia dell'arte* to Nichols and May. All have used the technique of improvisation as a means of entertainment. In the *commedia* they used prepared scenarios, about a hundred of which have been handed down and can be read to this day. Even though the plays were improvised, they had specific plots and specific characters—Pantalone, Harlequin, and so on. *Commedia* also provided a good instrument for anti-court propaganda. Because it was performed off the cuff and there was no evidence of anything written down that could be considered subversive, it was possible, while you were improvising your situation, to throw in a few impertinent digs at the King.

Mike Nichols and Elaine May were nightclub performers for some years and did a series of improvisations based on situations which they gave themselves and characters whom they chose. Sometimes they asked the audience to suggest situations and they improvised on those. Regardless of how "loose" it may have seemed to the people in the audience, there always was some form to their numbers. They themselves, being actors/directors/writers, had the idea that sketches had beginnings, middles, and ends. They knew, when they came to a good gag, to stop there, so they could end with a laugh. Or they prepared an ending which they worked toward. They had a sense of form even though they were improvising.

The Open Theatre, directed by Joseph Chaikin, had another technique, which was to arrive at the actual performance scripts through improvisation. The company would begin with a theme, would improvise on it, develop characters animal and human, and create sound effects. They would improvise and improvise until they found something that was usable and clear and entertaining and they would save that. Then they would work some more and save another piece, until finally they had what was virtually a play script and it could be written down. Actually, this kind of work had gone on for some time. In the Group Theatre much of the material of our plays was conceived similarly. For *Men in White*, for example, the whole boardroom scene was improvised and the author, Sidney Kingsley, sat in the auditorium and grabbed every good character line or good laugh and inserted it into the script. This kind of collaboration between actors and author is another use of improvisation in rehearsal.

One of the great values of improvisation is for training. Improvisation is the *control of the problem.* For "problem" you can substitute "intention." You do not ramble, you *execute the intentions* set either by you or the director, and the improvisation is the result of that execution. But now you are the author of the words, not Shakespeare or Tennessee Williams. Jazz musicians, when they get together to have a jam session, begin with some melody or musical idea that is the basis for their improvisation. Otherwise there would be a cacophony in no time at all. It would be noise, not a jam session. There are some strictures, some musical laws that are retained and that keep this "freedom"—which is all some people think improvisation is—from becoming anarchy and that give it some form, even though it's a free form. There always must be something to improvise *on*.

In painting there are strict forms and there are some forms that are so free they consist of dripping paint on the canvas. But if all you had to do was drip paint, anybody could be Jackson Pollock. Obviously anybody isn't. There must be something that is different. What is different is that Pollock, being an artist, had a built-in sense of form. Even though he found the freest way to apply his paint to canvas, he must have had some vision, even subconsciously, as to what the whole painting would be so that after he had finished dripping, that very freedom had an artist's structure to it. People who are not artists, without the innate sense of form and space, could drip the same paint on the same canvas and the result would be an absolute blur.

Let me lay out some of the values and possible dangers of improvisation. When you study any valuable technique, there are always dangers inherent in it that can and should be guarded against.

Improvisation, as a training aid, gives you a chance to study the process of intention—the feeling inside you that you are executing and controlling your objective. You are helped in this through improvisation because, when you are given dialogue, the author, in one way or another, has suggested what the intentions are and you, rightly or wrongly, feel that you are performing those objectives. When you have no dialogue at all, you are obliged to design your own inner line. And, when you are temporarily freed from the author's dialogue (repeat: temporarily), it allows you, it *forces* you to concentrate on your intentions. You've pared away everything but that inner line.

The second value of improvisation is to help you establish connection with your partner. This is good as a rehearsal technique. Sometimes the author's words fail to help you make that connection because they are not the words *you* would choose if you really had that intention toward this person. Therefore, you can leave the author's words for a few minutes and improvise. You first set for yourself the sections of the scene. "From here to here is where I realize there's something funny about her today; at this point I realize that she's lying and from that point I tell her to get the hell out." Those are the three actions that should happen. If you know the inner design and you improvise on that, you create that situation in your own words. It's like expressing your subtext more naturally. The author's lines may be foreign to you in some way, abstract or poetic, and that has hindered you in communicating with the other actor clearly. Now that you've got it in your words, go back to the author's lines *immediately* after you have established that connection with your partner and the dialogue will begin to adhere to that inner line you have just improvised upon.

Next value: to force talking *and* listening. What happens often in rehearsals of a play around the second or third week is that you've done the scenes over in so many ways and you know them so well that you're no longer really listening—I mean listening with intention—you are just "hearing." And you are not really talking any more—just delivering the lines. Talking is the result of your having some wish to convey to your partner or object and now this wish seems to have disappeared. This also happens sometimes after the play has opened and played for a while. The actors get into a "pattern" of playing. They know the cues and the lines and the moves and where the laughs are so they no longer do the basic work which created that pattern in the first place. Talking and listening are two things *without which you cannot do,* from the first reading to the last performance. By going back to improvising a scene, you are forced to listen because you don't quite know what the person is going to say. You are forced to talk and think because you're no longer repeating the author's lines but are expressing the character's wishes and thoughts in your own words.

Improvisation also helps you to develop a sense of the "first time," one of the sine qua nons of acting. An audience should not sense that it is witnessing an entertainment which has been very carefully rehearsed for its delectation and applause, but rather that it is seeing something that is transpiring at that very second for the first time. That quality of the first time, unfortunately, is very rare among actors. It requires knowing what you're doing, plus the ability to forget it and then to find it again when you get on stage. The truly great actors have that gift. It was certainly one of the hallmarks of Laurette Taylor. In *Outward Bound,* by Sutton Vane, she entered a bar on a ship in which all the characters were dead (as was she) but were unaware of it. On her first entrance she came on *really* lost. She didn't know who these people were, where she was, what she was doing there. Of course you sat right forward in your seat because *you* knew and you almost wanted to get up there to help her. You wanted to say, "It's all right, darling. It's just that you're dead." The alternative is the actor who comes on and *indicates* he is lost. You sit back in your seat because you know that he knows he is lost. It's an entirely different experience for an audience. With fine actors, we are involved. With any great performer you don't sit back and analyze the action while it's going on. You might analyze it later, but you have an experience while it's happening. The great actors seem to be improvising as they're playing.

Another rehearsal use of improvisation is to develop some element of characterization that doesn't come out of your work on the part. Suppose you had to play a coal miner in a play which had no scene in a coal mine. Let's say it all took place in the kitchen; it was a family play about a coal miner, his wife and children. The wife keeps warning him of the dangers of mine work. She's never sure he'll come home from work alive. The actor playing the miner has no chance to develop the character elements that make it believable to the audience that this man works eight hours a day in the mines. You might be very truthful as husband, father, and breadwinner, but the director, sitting out there in the house, may say: "It's fine what you're doing but I somehow don't believe you were ever in a mine." There are then things that you can do with improvisation to develop those elements and make your characterization more fully believable.

A director can give you a good improvisation in which you are in a very low tunnel of a coal mine for an exploration. This obliges you to get down on your knees and it may be the first time in rehearsal you have gotten down on your knees. In the improvisation you have to crawl a long way toward a small speck of light you can barely see in the distance. If you're doing it well, the improvisation will expose you to certain rigorous physical problems. Try it and you'll see how you feel when you stand up. If you've been kneeling and crawling for five minutes and know how that feels, you can imagine how it would feel after eight hours and after thirty years. You know now what happens to your whole body, including the grime that gets into your skin and never gets out. It involves what happens to your eyes when you can't quite see and what happens when the coal dust gets into your mouth and your nose and where exactly your back hurts. Everything begins to change now. You no longer play the part as if you were a bank clerk. You have a sense of the character's physical life. But beyond that, the improvisation can be developed further. The director might say: "When I clap my hands, there is a cave-in at the end of the tunnel and the exit is shut off. You can't get out." In other words, some psychological problem is added—the element of danger. What do you do to get out in a situation like that? And what do you do if you don't get out? What is that death like?

If you worked well on that improvisation, then it's a whole different kettle of fish in that scene, after a day's work, when you simply have to enter the kitchen, hang up your hat, see the table set for dinner and your wife looking at you as if to say, "You're late. I didn't know if you were dead or alive." All the elements of characterization, inner and physical, which make the character specifically a miner and not simply a father, are part of you now.

Now a word about the dangers. When badly done, improvisation can encourage a lack of form—and that's certainly one thing we don't have to encourage. We have that in spades. If, for instance, you are improvising a scene from a play you're rehearsing in order to regain some lost freshness and you wander away from the form of the scene, start to ramble on with inappropriate material, or stray from your character, that kind of "freedom" can distort your understanding of the ingredients of the scene rather than clarify it.

Another danger of doing lots and lots of improvisations is that it can tend to encourage a disrespect for the author's lines. In other words, in improvisation you say it the way you would like to say it, the way it's comfortable for you, the way it comes trippingly on *your* tongue. But in a play you're not yourself, you're the character. And you're bound in by the particular phraseology of the author, the sentiments of his language, verse if it's verse, or rhymed if it's a Molière couplet. Even if it's a twentieth-century play about the South by Tennessee Williams, you have an entirely different kind of language to cope with than with a play taking place in roughly the same locale by William Inge. If the use of improvisation levels all this out, then you have used the technique to a destructive end. The help you get from improvising the play's situation should make you say the author's lines better, not alter them in some way so they no longer represent his sound or his character in that situation or in that time or place.

I had an actor in rehearsal once who said, "Y'know," before every line. He couldn't start to talk without saying, "Y'know." He also had a little hand gesture to go with it. I said, "There are no 'Y'knows' in that speech. What's going to happen when you have to say, 'To be or not to be'? Are you going to say, 'Y'know, to be . . .'? You may think of it as a lesser sin to do that to this author than to Shakespeare, but I don't. You either respect the work you're doing or you don't. If you're an artist, you don't play Beethoven's little Minuet in G with less musicianship than his great C Minor Sonata. You don't say, 'This is just realistic dialogue. If I can say it my way, it'll be more natural.' " That's a wrong definition of truth. That's personal truth and has nothing to do with artistic truth. That's one of our big problems these days.

If you are going to use improvisation as a helpful technique in rehearsing a scene, you have to remember the following application—and if you don't, you're going to get into trouble. You check over the sections, or intentions, of the scene carefully. Now you improvise it. You don't make it a different play. You do *this* scene but in your own words. The second after you finish the improvisation—and I mean the *second:* you don't go to lunch, you don't have a cigarette, you don't talk about it—go right back to the beginning of the scene and do it with the author's lines. The inner pattern of the sections that you have established in your head is fresh in your mind. The values of connection, relation to the partner, sense of talking and listening, etc., that you developed improvisationally should adhere to the actual scene. Maybe not all of it will, but then that's a subject for discussion after you've finished the scene. You might then say, "In that last part of the improvisation I seemed to realize that she didn't care whether she was going to live or not." The director might reply, "That was very good in the improvisation. I don't want to lose that. You can keep that intention going in your whole last speech."

It's quite possible that in the improvisation you get a little moment like that that enriches the inner life of the dialogue and that you might never have discovered without improvisation. But, whatever happens, it all has to do with working within the form. It doesn't, however, mean you have to be dogmatic about sticking to a structure or that once you decide on one, you never change it. Everything in acting is creating and creative. During the whole rehearsal process the inner line is a living, changing thing. It's the *sense* of form I'm talking about. I must say that even after the play opens, there's a certain amount of freedom still there that keeps the playing improvisational in quality even though you now know the lines, the moves, everything. I go back to a play periodically and suggest something here or there for the actors to try that won't change the basic nature of the scene but is another way of doing it—a nuance that might give the actors something to think about. If they do, oddly enough, all the material around that moment becomes fresher too, because the actor knows he has something slightly different he's going to do that night. In this way, without changing the basic pattern, you can keep a performance alive.

Let me finish with a classic example of one of the dangers inherent in improvisation (in this case a group improvisation): an actor pursuing his own intention so relentlessly that an impasse is reached. It happened in 1933 in the Group Theatre rehearsals of Sidney Kingsley's *Men in White.* Lee Strasberg, the director, laid out an improvisation for the whole cast as preparatory work for the all-important operating room scene in the play. We were each given characters in the improvisation similar to those we were cast for. The scene was the O.R. and the little amphitheatre surrounding the operating area where interns or visiting doctors could observe. Morris Carnovsky was the chief surgeon performing the delicate operation and one of our best actors, Luther Adler, was a famous visiting Viennese doctor observing the operation.

After the washing up and putting on of masks and gloves, Morris stepped up to the patient lying on the table and called out, "Scalpel." The efficient nurse slapped the knife into the surgeon's hand and he poised it carefully over the chosen spot on the abdomen. Just as Morris was on the point of making the incision, Luther called out, "Excuse me, Doctor, but the patient is dead." We could see Morris fuming under his mask because he hadn't even gotten started on his task. Summoning all the logic he could under the circumstances, he bent down, studied the patient carefully, turned to Luther, and said, as politely as he could (after all, Luther was playing a famous European surgeon), "Doctor, it's quite possible that, from where you're sitting, it appears that way, but I assure you the patient is alive." With that, he lifted his scalpel again and brought it down with determination on the abdomen. "I'm sorry, Doctor," said Luther, quite calmly, "he's dead." Now doing a slow burn, Morris turned to the anaesthesiologist and said, "Doctor, would you please check the patient's pulse and breathing?" Sandy Meisner, the able attending physician, went through a careful routine of checking all vital signs. "He's still with us, Doctor," said Sandy, implying, "He *won't* be if you don't get going." Smiling triumphantly at Luther, Morris carefully laid the point of his scalpel on the patient's stomach and prepared to cut. "He's dead," said Luther.

Well, at this point, Strasberg blew his top. Stopping the improvisation, which was grinding to a halt anyway, he pointed out in his famous, arctic manner, although this time he was eminently right and was teaching us an important lesson, that the point of an improvisation, as of a scene, is *to make it happen,* not to make it *not* happen. Even if Luther had had the greatest justification in the world for himself, theatrical logic demands that one's intentions be adjusted to the needs of the scene and to the whole truth around one and not be purely arbitrary.

EXERCISE:

Here's an improvisation that ensures the process of talking and listening. It's a telephone set-up. I am going to place these two chairs about two feet apart *with their backs to each other.* Each chair is in a room in a separate location by a telephone. I want one person to go to the telephone and call up someone in the class. When that actor hears his or her name, he will go to the other chair and answer the phone. You are each then in different places talking on the telephone. The first actor should have a definite purpose (objective) in mind, preferably something strong, urgent, imaginative. Don't just call your friend and ask her to go to the movies: that isn't likely to lead to a great confrontation. Have a clear intention, stick to it in whatever logical ways you can in order to fulfill it. The person receiving the call, upon hearing the request, demand, favor, or whatever, that is put to him, should immediately adopt *his* intention and pursue it with all the logic at his command. The dialogue resulting from the two people on the telephone, each *controlling* his own objective, will constitute the improvisation. Let's have a volunteer with something interesting in mind. . . .

Notes after the exercise:

Don't anticipate. You immediately refused to give him the five grand he asked for. Do your fellow students usually call you up in the morning for a loan of $5,000? I, for one, would, first of all, be flattered. You see, it is not only enough to play your action (which probably would have been "to refuse the nut"); you must create the *logic* of the situation, not simply accept it. Maybe you'd first try to find out if he's kidding. If he isn't, how the hell did he get into a spot where he needed that much money at once? If it seems genuine, and he's your crazy friend, even though you have to refuse him because you haven't got the money to lend, you might try to think of some suggestion as to where he might go, etc., etc. You then are dealing with a situation based on the truth of your relationship, your characters, the circumstances, and so on, and not playing your intention abstractly.

EXERCISE:

Let me have Maxine and Mike. The scene of this improvisation is Maxine's apartment. The two of you are "just friends." Maxine is home and Mike is going to come to her apartment. This is not unlike the telephone improvisation except that you are together in person in the same room. In other words, Mike's overall action is to request, even demand, something from Maxine which she, for her own reasons, will refuse. . . .

Notes after the exercise:

I couldn't quite hear you. How about that? Here I am, roughly ten feet from you. You had *life* energy, just about enough to communicate with each other if you were really in a room and not in a room on the stage. This is one of the bad habits one can get into doing improvisations. If you feel low in energy before you start, energize! Do a couple of those exercises we did in the beginning. They are not only for study, but to be used when needed in performance. If you have good energy and play your actions clearly and strongly, we will never have to say, "Speak up." And a good thing, too, because if you just raise your voice, it might make you sound false. You get more volume either by having more energy or by altering your intention to something stronger.

Now for scenic truth. If someone knocked on your door as Mike did, would you, Maxine, sitting on your bed like that, call out, "Come in"? Not even a "Who's there?"—in New York City yet? Don't always take the easy way. Your door wasn't even locked. Create your environment with some imagination. Otherwise you are in some kind of physical limbo and your inner life gets washed out too, through disbelief. And be aware of the mundane details of everyday life— like asking, "Who is it?" An audience may not take note of them if they're there but will be entirely aware of their absence if you overlook them.

Mike, when she refused you, you got angry at her immediately, bawled her out, and behaved in a way calculated to ensure that you would *never* get what you wanted. Since you say your overall action in the scene was to get her to comply, you were not *controlling the problem* but changing it. That's what comes from playing the emotion but not the action. There's nothing wrong with your getting upset at the difficulties she was creating, but, angry or not, your job in the scene was to get her to do what you wanted. Your anger might have caused you to trick her in some hideous way to do your bidding; that's Okay. You'd still be solving the problem of your improvisation. The value of this exercise is to learn to control—in whatever way you can invent—your objectives and not be pulled away by any force, especially emotion.

EXERCISE:

Here's a favorite confrontation: the president of the university and the head of the student committee. The scene is the president's office. The student comes in and presents a list of demands. Susan, you are the president. Bill, you are the newly elected chairman of the student committee. I'll take you each aside for your battle instructions.

(Aside to Bill) You were entrusted, after a stormy meeting the night before, to submit a list of demands—I leave the particulars to you—to the president and not to take no for an answer. Your action is "to insist on these demands, or else."

(Aside to Susan) You have compromised, as much as you decently could while still preserving the university, with previous demands of former heads of student committees. This one, you've been told, is a born troublemaker. Your action is "to draw the line at any demand so unreasonable as to imperil the rest of the university." . . .

Notes after the exercise:

The big issue here is one of *adjustment.* Adjustment means just that: how you adjust to particular circumstances, environments, characters, etc. If you enter the New York Public Library, the imposing size of the place, the countless rows of books, the people sitting around reading and studying, all have an automatic effect on you. If you've been talking, you lower your voice. You also adjust differently to a baby than you do to an adult, and still differently to a sick baby. Now, come on, I don't care how much of a radical you're playing, Bill, she's still the president of the university and not the cheerleader of the football team. I don't even know how you got in there so easily. I was chairman of the Acting and Directing Departments of the Yale School of Drama and *I* never even barged into Dean Brustein's office like that, much less President Kingman Brewster's. Even if you try to justify it on emotional grounds, something would have had to be made of such an unbelievable entrance. Secretarial heads, at least, would roll. And that same unbelievability pervaded the entire improvisation because you seemed to be equals, fighting in general, not from the point of view of your characters. One wonders at the constituency that voted such an impolitic boor to be its representative. It all comes from playing intentions in a vacuum, instead of in the circumstances and according to the relationship of the characters. Worse still, it comes from "playing yourself" instead of the play. You musn't seek out the truth by asking yourself what *you* would do in that situation. You must ask, "What would I do if I were *that character* in that situation?" Later on, when we discuss the problems of style, we'll add "in that play, by that author, in that period, of that class, etc., etc." We must use our sense of truth to serve the material (even in improvisations), not ourselves.

EXERCISE:

This is an improvisation involving a specific element of characterization as well as our usual problem of intention. The scene is a watchmaker's shop. Paul, you will be the watchmaker and, in a moment, I'll ask you to set up your shop with all the props that are characteristic of such a shop and such an artisan. Carolyn, you are a customer who comes into the shop. I'm going to take you each aside and whisper the circumstances leading up to the scene (the given circumstances) and your individual objectives.

Then we'll start with the watchmaker working in this shop; after a few moments the customer will enter.

(Aside to Paul) Weeks and weeks ago this dame brought in a rare antique Swiss watch with a broken mainspring. You, an expert craftsman, tried all over to find a mainspring to fit it. Finally you had to order one from Switzerland. After an eternity, it arrived—but way downtown at the customhouse where you had to go to bail it out. At last you put the mainspring in the damn thing, got the watch to go, called the customer. She came yesterday, paid the handsome amount you had to charge her, and left with her repaired watch. Now here she is, back again. Your intention: "to refuse to be saddled with that troublesome watch again."

(Aside to Carolyn) Weeks ago, you brought this gorgeous

family heirloom (it was your grandmother's watch) in to this highly recommended watchmaker because it had stopped. He kept it forever. Each time you called, he had some reason why it wasn't ready. Finally you picked it up yesterday. He charged you an arm and a leg. Since it was so precious to you, you had to pay up, happy to have it back and going once more. No sooner had you gotten home than the watch stopped again and you couldn't get it going. So here you are back at the shop. Your intention: "to make him take that watch back and fix it properly for the fortune you paid him."

Notes after the exercise:

First, scenic truth. It was good that you improvised a magnifying glass to fit in your eye, Paul. But that was to be expected in the character of a watchmaker. However, I wished that your handling of your props before and during the customer's visit had made us believe more in your characterization of the expert craftsman. When you hit that delicate, defenseless heirloom on your table because you had difficulty opening the back of it, I nearly went into cardiac arrest— which, incidentally, is where the customer should have gone, too, instead of blandly accepting this mayhem. The belief in what you do includes the belief in all the physical life around you, too. I also wondered, when you, Carolyn, pulled that poor naked heirloom out of your bag where it could have been scratched by lipstick, or God knows what, why you hadn't wrapped it up in a bit of protective tissue paper. Don't just accept things, *create* the truth of them through your understanding of all the ingredients of your situation and with the use of your imagination.

About the confrontation, now. I won't complain about your asking him for your money back, Carolyn, although it wasn't exactly going to fulfill your objective of getting him to take the watch back and fix it properly. At least it was a spinoff on that intention when you seemed to reach an impasse and you didn't want it to be a total loss. But, again, when he said no, you capitulated at once. What about threatening legal action? The Better Business Bureau? Invent logical developments, don't settle so easily.

And Paul, you gave her good reasons why you couldn't spend your life with this watch. But, again, don't only pursue the intention of refusing to take it back from *your* point of view but, by active listening, use material *she* is giving you to further fulfill your objective. For example, when she said, "It just stopped," why believe her? Maybe she dropped it. In other words, let's always think of intention as a two-way street. Not: I am doing mine and you are doing yours and the two actions pasted together equal a scene. Rather: *As* I play my intention I connect so with my partner that I see how my action is landing on him or her and this communion is what gives the special life to my inner action. Then, as I listen, I don't just hear what my partner says in order to get ready to slap him with my next intention but I listen, actively, with an awareness of how what I am hearing fits in with my ongoing inner line and is, indeed, a continuation of it. That is what I meant in my intention talk about the FLUIDITY of the subtext.

EXERCISE:

The scene of this improvisation is the office of a well-known producer. An actor comes in and applies for a part in a production the producer is preparing. Ken, you'll be the actor and Julius, you be the producer. I'll give you your instructions separately.

(Aside to Ken) Your action is "to get that part you know you can play magnificently." Through your agent, who had a copy of the script, you've read the play and there is a character in it tailor-made for you. You also happen to know the part is still open because a friend of yours has been been up to the office about it and reported to you that none of the actors the director has seen has satisfied him.

(Aside to Julius) You know this actor by reputation. You've been told, not only by other producers but by your stage manager, that this guy is bad news. He's reported to be a first-class troublemaker. They say he not only complains forever about working conditions, rehearsal hours, the other actors, and so on, but he's been known to go crying to Equity about the slightest infractions on the part of management. Your objective, then, is "to keep this troublemaker out of the production," without, of course, revealing your reasons. You don't want to be hauled up for discriminatory labor practices. . . .

Notes after the exercise:

I'm going to bring you both up on charges. Not to Equity or the League of New York Theatres, but to Aristotle for your abuse of logic. You see, it's not enough to pursue your intention. You must pursue your intention *with logic.* It's no use, Ken, making the producer feel like a liar, even if you do think he's not telling you the real reasons why he wants to turn you down. You may be right, but you'll never, never get the part that way and *that's* your objective. And, Julius, in your powerful position, there must be easier ways to get this fellow out of your office than by descending to his level of acrimony. The producers I remember turning me down were always heartbroken. Anyway, the point is not only the pursuit of your intention but the *way* that pursuit is developed. And that depends on the use of logic in the application of your *circumstances.*

EXERCISE:

This will be a group improvisation. Let me have ten volunteers. Now these four chairs mark out the space of an elevator in the World Trade Center. These two front chairs indicate the door of the elevator. The ten of you have each gotten on at different floors above and the last local stop was the sixtieth floor. From there on down to the lobby it is an express. When the improvisation starts, the elevator has left the sixtieth floor and is on its way to the bottom. When I bang my hand on the table, that is a signal that the elevator grinds to a halt and is stuck between two floors, where it remains. I want each of you to decide for yourselves who you are, what you were doing in the building before you boarded the elevator, and where you were going when the trouble struck. . . .

Notes after the exercise:

Not too bad, although some of you could have invented more crucial situations—places that you had to be urgently, important items that had to be delivered at once, conditions of health that this situation would exacerbate, and so on. Bland choices make bland acting. The main criticism I would have, though, is the fact that many of you, although dealing well with your own problems (or, in the case of those who teamed up, your partners' problems), didn't do as well with the whole group. You tended to let others fend for themselves, like the guy who obviously (*we* guessed it early and you all were standing right next to him!) had some dangerously explosive material in his little suitcase. Believability was further strained by the roughness with which he was handled. Most inventive was Marcell as the poor lady in the back with the hysterical monkey on a chain who finally misbehaved on the floor. I could feel your sense of relief when I mercifully called an end to the improvisation!

EXERCISE:

Here we are at gibberish. Instead of real words, you are to speak your "dialogue" using crazy, mixed-up words and sounds. The way you make yourself understood, of course, is by the clarity with which you express your intentions to your partner. Some actors' gibberish sounds vaguely French or German or whatever, depending on their individual proclivities. Some speak in unidentifiable combinations of unrelated vowels and consonants. My gibberish leans toward the Russian, I think. If I want Brock to stand up, for example, I might say, "Prostcheye, Bruski, schtay ovni." You notice how I helped myself, unconsciously, with an expressive look and demonstrative gestures I probably wouldn't have needed had my words been enough. But this inner urge to get your intention across clearly is the point of this gibberish improvisation. It is an exercise in the mastery of your "inner line."

The scene is a doctor's office. Martha, you are a patient coming to this doctor for help. Brian, you are the doctor trying to help her. Come over here, one at a time, and I'll give you further instructions.

(Aside to Martha) You have been given his name and told he is a reputable psychiatrist. You have had emotional problems (I leave specifics to you) that have left you unable to cope any more and, fearful of a complete nervous breakdown, you have looked this doctor's address up in the phone book and come to him for much-needed help.

(Aside to Brian) You are a very fine gynecologist. . . .

Notes after the exercise:

That was very funny. I particularly liked the moment where, when he asked her to take her clothes off, she, obviously having gained her knowledge of psychiatrists from paperbacks, speculated for a moment as to how he was going to get at her psyche that way—and finally decided not to comply. The only complaint I might register (to keep my franchise as a teacher) is to remark that it is wise *to know when you are finished.* I stopped you when the impasse reached started to repeat itself and stretch out. When the point came that you both realized something was desperately mistaken in this encounter, either the doctor has to end the consultation or the patient has to get the hell out.

EXERCISE:

Probably none of you is old enough to remember when Mike Nichols and Elaine May performed their improvisations. One of their standards was to ask the audience to call out three disparate words on which the two of them could build an improvisation. Actually, Mike and Elaine were too young to know that in the early thirties we Group Theatre actors did that same exercise in Lee Strasberg's class. And now *we're* about to try it. I am going to ask this group to suggest three words, in no way related to each other. Then two actors will decide what their characters are, where the scene takes place, and what the situation is. Just be sure that somewhere the three chosen words turn up—either in the dialogue itself or implied in the setting, a prop, or by any other means. I'm ready for suggestions. . . . Okay. Let's settle for "cucumber," (nuclear) "fission," and "Pope." . . .

Notes after the exercise:

Your sense of invention was fine. And all the words were there. What we need to think about a bit more is our sense of the scenario. Did you decide, before you started, on the sections—the beginning, the middle, and the end? That is not to say that whatever you laid out could not have been altered in the course of the improvisation. But there would have been a form to alter—not a blind groping to get to the revelation of the next word (which was cleverly done, by the way. I don't mean the groping, but the believable way you worked the three words in). It's this sense of *inner form* (just as important, we always say, in improvisations as in scenes) that we have to emphasize. Nichols and May, having the additional problem of entertaining an audience, were always sure to recognize the need for a good finish, either accidentally come upon or decided in advance.

EXERCISE:

Here's an assignment that I want you to prepare at home and bring in to class. It is designed to prove to you how you can infuse any line with whatever meaning you wish by the execution of your chosen intention. I want you to take a line of poetry, place it in a situation other than that which is suggested by the words' meaning, choose a character or be yourself, give the line a clear intention, again quite removed from what the line suggests, and then perform it. What's more, I want you to choose five different circumstances and intentions for the same line to develop your understanding that a line reading is determined not only by the sense of the words but by what is *intended* by your character in a situation.

I'll give you an example. Suppose I chose for my line of poetry Mrs. Browning's "How do I love thee? Let me count the ways." I am a cop in the police station questioning a young hood I brought in. He has just called me a pig. I grab him by his shirt front with my left hand and, wanting "to take care of this punk" (my intention), with my right hand I slap his face on both sides as I say the first half of the line and knee him in the groin on the second half. Like this (grabbing him): "How do I love *thee*?" (slap) "Let me count the ways" (kneeing the groin). Mrs. Browning might be a bit surprised, but notice that I didn't *ignore* her words and gabble them over just to play my new meaning. I tried to *use* her words to help convey the meaning.

Now I am no longer a cop taking care of a punk. I am the foreman of a firm of outdoor sign painters standing on Broadway looking high up at a scaffolding hanging on a building. On it is a painter making one of those huge cigarette signs. The name of the cigarette is emblazoned across an idyllic scene of a romantic couple lying in a field, with the guy saying to the gal, "How do I love thee? Let me count the ways." Only the schlemiel who's painting, instead of printing WAYS has spelled it LAYS. I scream up at him, in order "to correct the idiot" (my intention), "How do I love thee? Let me count the WAYS!!"

I am still using Mrs. Browning's dialogue but, obviously, this is a completely different situation and a completely different objective. I want you to prepare five of these to go with one chosen line of poetry. I'll see them next time.

Notes after the exercise:

Some of the intentions you chose were quite clearly played. In a couple of cases, they weren't. You chose a beautiful line from Robert Frost and twice *his* original meaning seems to have won out. I'll tell you what you can do to ensure the infusing of the line with the intention *you* have chosen. First, improvise your inner action in your own words, retaining your character and situation. (Keep it the same length as your line of poetry.) Then, immediately after, repeat the same intention, only this time with Robert Frost's text.

VARIATION:

Another assignment. Choose a short poem of about eight or ten lines. Treat it like a speech in a play. Decide where it is taking place, what your character is, and place your character in a situation. Then choose an overall action and break it down into smaller actions. We will see how your choices enhance, destroy, or comment on the original sense of the poem. For Lee Strasberg, in the Group Theatre, I once did Walt Whitman's paean to the human body, "I sing the body electric." I played a shivering old guy getting out of a warm bed in the morning and stepping into what was obviously a freezing cold shower. As the first blast of icy liquid hit him, he screamed out in pain the first line: "I sing the body electric!" Then, as he quickly soaped, rinsed, and dried each section of his shaking body, I went from organ to organ as praised so lavishly by Mr. Whitman, choosing my inner and outer actions to make my own comments on the text. At the end, my tortured man leaped back under the blankets. It turned out funny enough to be used as a number for all those benefits we played during the Depression.

Notes after the exercise:

I want you to do that one again. Next time, don't let so many of the words lapse into a sort of gibberish used merely to express your intention. See how many of your poet's words can *add* to the verification of your situation or be used to create an opposite impression or a comment. This is fine preparation for clarifying texts with difficult, even abstruse, verse.

Work on Roles

I always have two things in my head—I always have
a theme and the form. The form looks for the theme,
theme looks for the form, and when they come together, you're able to write.

—W. H. Auden

You all have chosen your scenes to work on. I am going to see
each one at least four times at the crucial points in your
rehearsal period: the first reading (beginnings are always important), the production talk (I am going to ask you, the
actors, to prepare it, although it's usually the province of the
director), after you have broken your scene down into its
sections, and, finally, staged, on your feet, using substitute
props, necessary elements of costume, etc. You will get notes
each time you are up and if, after the last of your four appear-
ances, we feel you can still get more out of your scene, we'll
have a final farewell performance. In this way we can follow
the progress of your work on the part throughout a simulated
rehearsal period and I can tell just where each of you tends
to go off. Some actors never do a good first reading. Trouble
in the third week of rehearsal can often be traced back to
this. They never really knew the play well enough. Others,
who may be fine in the early around-the-table rehearsals,
develop hang-ups when it comes to characterization. If you
prepared your scene by yourself and just presented it, as is
so often done in "scene-study" classes, it would be difficult to

tell, if something were out of kilter, at just what stage of rehearsal you goofed off. The best I could do would be, like a critic, to tell you what I feel is wrong with your scene and ask you to do it over. That has some value, of course, but I would rather try to approximate the work of director and actor as they prepare the performance together.

The amount of time one takes with each section of the rehearsal period alters, of course, according to the nature of the script. If it is a deeply psychological play with an involved subtext, more time is spent in the chairs, digging out the intentions, relationships, and feelings of the characters. But if you're preparing a wild farce, where the dialogue is only a frothy topping for the physical movement—where, indeed, the "meaning" consists of getting your behind through that door just before the jealous husband can catch you—you'd better get up on your feet and work it out pretty soon. Since your characterization will most likely be fairly physical, it will be more fun for you to do this work in movement, rather than sitting around the table pondering it.

Mind you, the first reading isn't always the first rehearsal. Sometimes the director likes to have one person read the play to the entire cast at the opening get-together. Some actors may worry about this, as they fear they may be shown how to play their parts. And, of course, if the play is read that way, the actors should worry. The reader should attempt simply to get the *points* of the play over, clearly, with no reaching for characterization or emotion. The person reading the play could be the director, it could be the author. (Some playwrights, not all, read their plays well. Arthur Miller is a fine reader of his own plays. You can hear him and he doesn't attempt to indicate performances.)

The values are these: the entire cast has heard the whole play. If you are reading your part in the very first rehearsal, chances are your concentration is so much on getting your own speeches out in time that you may not have really absorbed the lines of the other characters, which is important for your complete understanding of the play *and* your part. Also, the entire cast has heard *one* play and, therefore, can start out on the same foot when they pick up their parts to read in what would then be the *second* rehearsal. Otherwise you sometimes get a variety of first reactions to the text, tending to fog up the play's meaning. Finally, the normal tensions of a cast meeting for the first time are done away with. By the time you, the actors, do your first reading, you have been together a whole morning, had lunch, and are now more relaxed with each other for your first reading together. Now, let's have a couple with their scene. Sit at this table where you can see each other clearly and we'll have your first reading.

First Readings

What should the actor aim for in his very first reading aloud of his part? Let me tell you two things you should *not* worry about. First, you should not worry about emotion. If a scene requires you to be crying uncontrollably or laughing hysterically, the only way you can indicate those feelings at this stage is just that way: indicating—or faking them. Since you don't want your work to be false at any stage, don't strain for emotional results you are not ready to achieve. Now, as soon as I've said that, I must modify it at once. If some situation in the play *does* move you as you read aloud for the first time or does strike you as hilariously funny, don't try *not* to feel. In other words, it's just as false to try not to feel something that is arrived at naturally as it is to force a feeling that is not there. The main point is not to worry about emotion at this time.

The second element you don't have to be too anxious about is characterization. If your part calls for an Italian accent and you don't have one handy, don't approximate it with some phony "datsa bigga t'ing" kind of garbage. That's not going to help the "belief in what you do" that we keep working for. You'll study the particular accent (not some generalized stuff) required for your part and work it into your dialogue as you rehearse. If you need to have an old man's voice and you're a young man, don't start with some high, creaky wheeze at once. After all, some old men have vibrant voices and some young men have veiled, ancient ones. So the best you can be doing is leaping at a cliché. Again, the moment I say this, I must allow for exceptions. (I'm not being perverse. I have never said anything about our craft without immediately being struck by all the possible contradictions. It's the nature of the beast.) If, for example, you were born in the South, were brought up with a South-ern-fried accent and, with the help of a diligent speech teacher, have "lost" it so you would not be typed, or limited, in casting, and now you have a part that requires a Southern accent, you can probably lapse into one with no sweat at all, just as you do when you go home for the holidays. One whiff of that magnolia and it all comes rushing back. If that's the case, it would be silly to avoid, or postpone, something that can be accomplished with so much ease that it does not interfere with what you should be concentrating on in your first reading.

And what is that? Well, that is TALKING and LISTENING. It sounds easier than it is. By talking I don't mean just speak-ing your lines, or reading them aloud, or, God forbid, mum-bling them. I mean conveying some intention to your part-ner. (Your partner usually is one other person, but not necessarily. Even if you're doing a monologue where, even-tually, you are going to be talking to yourself as a partner, it is helpful, at first, to use other actors as a partner so you have someone to connect with.) Now you say, how the hell do I know what my intention is, this is just my first reading? You may not know exactly. The ultimate choices of your objectives will come as the rehearsals progress. But you do know the play, something of your character and the situation. Looking now at your lines, you can guess what *might* be intended by what you say. That's enough. It will ensure that you are talking, conveying some point to your partner, connecting with him and not with your script. You should also, as you are talking, see how what you are saying is landing on your partner. This guides *how* you talk and prevents you from just throwing your line (even with intention) at your partner, letting him grab it how he will as you pore over your next line coming up. Don't worry about pauses, picking up cues, etc. This is not a performance, it's an early rehearsal. You won't bore us if you pause a second to arrive at some intention before you speak. Work is never boring—gabbling is.

Next, listening. Just as talking is not the same as speaking, listening is not the same as hearing. I mean listening *with intention.* Here, too, even if you are uncertain as to exactly what you are doing (inside) as you listen, you can at least listen in order to find out what the other guy means by what he is saying. That will ensure the continuation of inner action until your next speech and will prepare you for your choice of intention when you do come in. This is active listening. So if you really talk and listen, connecting with your partner, in your first reading, you are actually acting from the beginning, in the sense that the basic principles of acting are present on some level. The proper choices, the corrections, come as you rehearse. When actors don't talk and listen at the first rehearsal, but are busy trying to "characterize" or to "feel" without any connection with their partners, I find I have to spend days getting them back to a good first reading instead of getting on to the work that would lead them to true character and emotion.

All right, let's have the first scene.

Notes after the first reading:

Well, that seemed pretty good—what I could hear of it. Here I sit, all the way back in the first row, about eight feet from you, and I missed whole chunks of the dialogue. I understand that when you are not quite sure of what you are doing, your impulse is to hide behind a mumble. I remember one year when I spoke at the Neighborhood Playhouse graduation exercises, Hermione Gingold was the other speaker. Her address was brief, but pointed. She said, "I have but one piece of advice for you: SPEAK UP! If you are good, everyone will want to hear you. If you are no good, we might as well know it straight away." When actors say to me after an inaudible first reading, "Don't worry. When I'm sure of what I'm doing, I'll talk up. You'll hear me 'on the night,' " my blood freezes at these "famous last words." Because, guess what, you still can't hear them at the dress rehearsal. Panicky, you yell: "Louder. I can't hear you out here in the auditorium!" They then start to "project" and a great hollowness envelopes what was a lovely, truthful, if silent-movie, rendition of their part. I'd rather you feel a bit false now, if indeed having enough vocal energy to be heard eight feet away makes you feel false, until proper stage energy becomes second nature to you and is no longer a problem, than have you lose your precious sense of truth later in order to turn up your volume. Somewhere along the line, we have learned to equate truth with mumbling into our beards and falseness with good vocal energy. It's a crock.

Production Talk

The first reading is over and we are ready for a production talk. Some directors present their production plans right at the first get-together of the cast. I always think that if the actors have read the play aloud, they have a better point of reference with which to understand the director's ideas. I am going to ask you, the actors, to prepare your own production talks as your next assignment. First, because you may not always have a director who can lay out the elements of the proposed production in a way that will guide you in your choices as an actor. He may just know "what he wants." Second, even if you do get a comprehensive idea of the proposed production you are in, you still need to know how to plan your acting work so that your character not only fits in with the overall design but flourishes from the knowledge of it.

I am going to give you an organized way to set down in your part the information gleaned from the production talk, so you can refer to it as you make your moment-to-moment choices in the course of the next days of rehearsal. It is like your palette. It has the main colors on it from which you create the different shadings and combinations. I suggest you use the back page of your part for this. Then, later, you can write the specific actions of your scenes on the left page opposite your dialogue. Make "sides" for yourself, if your scene is in a book of the play. "Sides" are those approximately 6″ × 8″ pages stapled together with the dialogue (complete —not "cues" only) on one side. You will be happy to have your sides all nicely marked up when you get to the third week of rehearsal and you want to check back to some note you made earlier. Also, at that point, you know most, if not all, of your lines and it is easy to glance at your sides if you need prompting, without having to juggle with some huge hard-covered script-holder or book.

The first point in a production talk ought to be the theme of the play according to the present, proposed production. Mind you, there's not just a single possible theme for a play. We are speaking only of this, our production, of it. Let's say the director decides, or you do, in this scene class, that the theme of *Hamlet* is that corruption in high places leads to the disintegration of the society. Parenthetically, it is always good to explore parallel examples of the theme in today's world, so that even if you are doing the play in period (and not a rock *Hamlet*!) your point of view will be contemporary and you'll thereby bring the play closer to your audience.

Then, you may ask, if that is the theme of this production, what is the spine of the play—the overall objective of all the characters? It is usually something fairly general since it must apply to all the parts. Let's settle for "to try to survive in a corrupt society." Now we are ready to deduce what the spine of each of the characters is. (You, playing one part, need only write your own character's spine down on your back page.) The King's super-objective could be "to clear away all obstacles to the throne," Rosencrantz and Guildenstern's "to serve the King." In these ways, all the various persons in the play "try to survive in this corrupt society." What of Hamlet himself? "To probe for the truth" might be his main objective. In one scene, he's trying to trap his uncle so he can find out the truth of his father's death ("The Murder of Gonzago" scene). Elsewhere, he's testing whether Ophelia still loves him or is being prompted by her father. And so on. He even probes the value of life itself ("To be or not to be"). I want to call attention to my choice of the word "probe" in my suggested spine of Hamlet. I've said, in relation to the choice of intentions, that the way you put them to yourself is important. I could have said "to search for the truth." But "probe" has an edge to it that will not only lead to stronger and more active subdivisions but open the door to actual physical character elements too. "Search" has a blandness to it. Probing could lead to that incisive look of a detective studying a culprit or a surgeon exploring a wound.

Now that the director, or you, in this case, has enunciated what he thinks all the characters want in the play, it is a good time to reveal what his concept of the play is, the overall style of the production. The designers of the scenery, costumes, props—also the composer of the incidental music, if any—have by now been apprised of this concept and are busy, each in his own department, trying to realize it. The actors, too, will be making their choices, inner and outer, based on the particular image the director has chosen for his concept. If he comes up, for *Hamlet,* with "A Prison," or "A Concentration Camp," or "An Occupied Country" as his image of the milieu in which the corruption festers ("rank corruption, mining all within, infects unseen," Hamlet tells his mother—Act III, Scene iv), then just as the designers must know how to get that atmosphere into their drawings, the actors, too, must be guided by the concept in arriving at intentions and behavior fitting for it.

I must stop, for a minute, to tell you the story of the time when Harold Clurman, the director of Clifford Odets's *Rocket to the Moon,* instructed the witty designer Mordecai (Max) Gorelik in the play's concept. "You see, Max, this takes place in a dentist's office. But I don't want just a dentist's office. I want a place which seems to be enclosing all these people, pressing in on them. I want it to be like a womb, you understand, Max? A womb." "Well, I was there once," said Max, "but I didn't take any notes." I also want to point out that this was in the thirties, so the idea of conceptual theatre must not be thought to be somebody's recent invention. All artists have worked from concepts, even though the nomenclature may have changed. In the Group, we called it "long-distance mood." How's that for a fancy phrase? What it came down to, actually, was a style, or concept, that encased the whole production. Gorelik's physical production idea for all the scenes of conflict in *Golden Boy* was the hard, white overhanging light of a prize-fight ring. (The Bonaparte home was all warm, wine color.)

Next, what of the characters themselves? Do they have any behavioral characteristics that might be revealing of their particular psychology? I call these character elements. It's a little hard to define. What I don't mean is elements of character such as "noble," "proud," "shy," etc. What sort of *activity* might arise from being shy? Would one be unable to look people directly in the eye? That would be a character element. It would be a behavior that would reveal the inner quality: shyness. Let me give a couple of examples from life. Lefty Hough was business manager at Twentieth Century-Fox when I was there under contract in the early forties after the Group Theatre folded. Lefty fascinated me because as he walked over that huge Fox lot he'd say a cheerful "Hi" to every person he'd pass, accompanying the "Hi" with a smart little one-finger salute from his forehead. One day I couldn't stand it any more. I had to find out why he did it. I stopped him (after he had just saluted me) and asked, "Lefty, do you mind if I ask you something? I notice that you greet everyone you pass, wherever and whenever it may be. I can understand your doing it to some, but to *everyone*?" "Well," said Lefty, as if I should have known, "you never know who'll be head of the studio tomorrow!" *That,* my friends, is a character element. The combination of the "Hi" and the salute to every person was the *theatrical manifestation* of an inner state.

My old friend Billy Rose, who'd been around Chicago gangsters in their heyday, used to thrust his forefinger at you in a rat-tat-tat movement as he talked. Now if he had been accompanying a threatening speech with this revolver-like motion, it would be a natural gesture. But when he used it to punctuate "I want you to come to dinner at eight o'clock," it became a character element. In case you think from this example that a character element has to be a gesture of some sort, it doesn't. It can simply be an attitude. Billy Rose had another hangover from his Chicago days. I gave a large party for theatre people once when I lived in a house in New York City with a floorthrough space that held about 150. Billy came and, seeing the crowd, immediately pasted himself against the back wall and stayed there. People came to him, but all my efforts to pry him loose to join others at the party were of no avail. Finally, I asked him why he clung to the wall like that. "In a crowd like this, never get out in the center of the room," said Billy. "You're an open target." That stance of Billy's, then, constituted a character element.

When I played the pharmacist in Charlie Chaplin's *Monsieur Verdoux* who was asked to prepare a perfect poison (that wouldn't show up in an autopsy) for Verdoux's use on unsuspecting rich females, Chaplin, who was the director as well as the lead character, only said one thing to me. It was enough, though, and it was a character element. Charlie said, "Listen, Bobby, when this bloke talks, he doesn't just talk, he *lectures*." That was all I needed. (I often wish all directors, including myself, could be so succinct.) From this advice, I got my whole attitude, my way of talking (relishing the pronunciation of the Latin medical terms, etc.) and I even got the idea for my costume and make-up, professional eyeglasses and all.

So then, on your back page, underneath the "concept," enter any character elements that may occur to you at this stage or in the ensuing rehearsal period.

For those of you who may be thinking, "This is pretty early on for me to be worrying about character when I haven't even set the inner pattern of my intentions," I say the following: All artists have some form in mind as they create. It is what helps them in their step-by-step choices. So too, we, if we understand that our character is "always on," will immediately change simple entering to "making an entrance" and simple exiting to "making an exit."

I will go further. I'll suggest that underneath your entry of "character elements" you put "characteristic props," as they occur to you. I don't mean the ordinary, utilitarian props that go with the action, but props that are revealing of your character. If the part calls for you to smoke, a cigarette is a utilitarian prop. But someone who smokes with the longest cigarette holder in the world is revealing the foppishness of his part. Incidentally, what often happens is that if you rehearse with such a cigarette holder and it gives you the air of a fop, you might very well end up without the actual holder at all. The air with which you now hold your cigarette makes you appear to be smoking out of a long cigarette holder. You may not even need the prop for the desired effect. But the "characteristic prop" helped you in the rehearsal period.

Utilitarian props can also be transformed into characteristic props by their usage on the stage. Opera glasses hung around a dowager's neck because she's going to the opera that night are utilitarian. But when she lifts them to her eyes to peruse (and hopefully magnify) any possible imperfections in the face of the pretty young girl sitting opposite her at the pre-opera dinner party, *that,* my hearties, reveals character.

Underneath props, I'd put "characteristic elements of costume." The same principle operates here. If an Edwardian gentleman wears spats, they're a utilitarian article of dress. But if some old gent gets dressed with his spats on to go out on the back porch and bring the milk in because he doesn't want the world ever to suspect him of not being a gentleman, that's a characteristic element of costume. Hildegarde, wearing gloves to play her piano in public, is certainly revealing some element of character.

Make-up, too. Suppose you were to play an old lady who fancies herself a flirtatious ingénue. You might want to wear a wig of blond ringlets that you can toss enticingly at each man you see. The interesting result might be that the particular air and movement the ringlets give you is sufficient. After rehearsing a while with the ringlets, you may find that the characterization you get from practicing with them and then using ordinary gray hair is even more touching.

So all of these things on the back page of your part are guides to the choices you are going to make during the early stages of rehearsal as you break your part down into its inner sections (the next stage of the work). Incidentally, when the production talk with all these suggestions is over (whether the director has given it or, as in our case in class, you yourself have worked it out), you should read through the scenes again looking all the while in the text for the proof of your production ideas which, of course, you got out of your study of the text in the first place.

Laurence Olivier caused some consternation among some orthodox Stanislavskyites when he announced to members of the Actors Studio that he can't really get going on a part till he understands what the *nose* is. Now, of course, he didn't mean he was going to work with some nose putty at the first reading. He was talking, as any artist might, of having some image in mind toward which he would work. If he saw the character as having a patrician nose, for instance, his inner choices might veer toward "to look down at them" instead of "to realize they're inferior." Again, after the attitudes gleaned from his understanding of the profile of the part (both inner and outer characteristics) have become organic in his performance, Olivier may not ever have to reach for his nose putty, even at make-up time. The effect is there.

Here is the way your back page should look after you have filled it in with the suggestions gleaned from the production talk (see page 112):

Subtext

The rest of the first week of a typical four-week rehearsal period is devoted to uncovering the subtext (the intentions) of the scenes, as guided now by the general plan gleaned from the production talk.

A good plan to follow at this point is this: As you break

Back Page:

Theme of the Play:

Spine of the Play:

My Character's Spine:

Production Concept (or Style):

Character Elements:

Props (characteristic):

Costume (characteristic):

Make-up (characteristic)

---

your scene down into its component parts and as you get suggestions from your director in rehearsals, enter them on the page to the left of your dialogue in your sides. Write the main intention for the section in the column furthest from the dialogue and the small actions or activities in the column closest to the text. This way, when you are studying your part at home in the evening, you learn your lines and intentions together. The inner line of your part becomes inseparable from your dialogue and doesn't have to enter into your consciousness as a separate "order" when you are acting. (We'll discuss the middle column of your left page, which is used for special problems of emotion, later.)

Your movements can be written right next to the dialogue on the page containing the text.

Let's turn to our illustration of the bit from *Hamlet,* Act III, Scene ii. Earlier in this scene, you will remember, is Hamlet's advice to the players. After his final instructions, the actors leave to prepare for their performance of "The Murder of Gonzago" with Hamlet's inserted speech. Polonius, Rosencrantz, and Guildenstern enter and inform Hamlet that the King and Queen are ready to see the play. Hamlet dispatches the three of them to hurry the Players. And now he is alone on stage in the place where the important performance will take place.

From studying the scene between Horatio and Hamlet that follows, it appears that what Hamlet is doing all through it is "getting ready to spring the trap." I make a note of that in the first column on my left page. Since this is the final moment before the performance is to happen, Hamlet takes the opportunity to check the layout: where the Players will act, making sure the King and Queen can see the action clearly from where they'll sit; deciding where Hamlet, Horatio, and Ophelia will be; and so on. This being the first "small action" of "getting ready to spring the trap," I'll put it at the head of the third column of the left page.

Hamlet is now ready to get Horatio's help, which he needs for reasons to be exposed in the forthcoming dialogue: he needs his well-balanced friend to confirm what he will observe in the King's reactions. Therefore, when he now calls, "What, ho, Horatio!" he's not just summoning him for a conversation, or because he wants to discuss Horatio's exemplary character with him. He wants "to get his help." That makes a different-sounding "What, ho," and he is now not stuck with a static discussion of Horatio's virtues (rather late in their friendship for this and, in any case, certainly not the moment) but is using all this as the buildup "to prepare Horatio for the shocking set-up" he's arranged to trap the King. Thus, the scene is uncovered by the study of the text, plus what we feel is going on underneath the lines, or the subtext.

When you have completed this section of the Hamlet-Horatio exchange, draw a line across both pages, your internal "score" and your dialogue. You are now ready to break down the next section of the scene where the court assembles for the performance. (See Ill. on p. 116.) This work of designing the inner line of your part is done, I'm sure you understand, during the reading rehearsals of the play with the other cast members and as a result of such rehearsals. You don't just figure it out by yourself and enter it on your left page with the notion that your work is then over (see pages 116–117).

Staging

During the final days of the first week's rehearsals in chairs, as you are finding your subtext, you should begin to use whatever little movements are possible to smooth the transition to the feet. I don't mean getting up and ambling around in a kind of limbo. This sort of "movement without staging" may seem to be necessary to some actors as a sort of release. Forget it. Moving in a physical limbo can only lead to thinking in an inner limbo. Yes, do get up and go over and sit next to someone you have to be intimate with. Yes, touch them if you'd like to. Yes, take the time to simulate the dialing of the phone, the pouring of the drink. All this anticipates the timing of the actual movements when you get to the staging and, indeed, makes the actual staging a relief, rather than the shock it is if it comes after immobility in the chairs. But ambling around for "comfort," no.

When putting the actors on their feet, I usually just give strategic positions so that the characters are in positions conducive to enacting the scenes physically with the intentions achieved in the chairs. Smaller moves come naturally out of these objectives and can be adjusted or cleaned up later, once the movement achieved by the strategic placement and the natural patterns arrived at by the intentions are there. The most exact staging desired, even stylized movement, can then be designed, but the inside (subtext) and the outside (movement) have been arrived at together without the latter being imposed arbitrarily on the former. After the whole play has been put on its feet, it is a good idea to go back and do each scene, or section of a scene, in the chairs once again to refresh the actors' minds as to their intentions, and then immediately do the same section on the feet to check the validity of the positions.

You are now ready for run-throughs without sets, costumes, props, etc. Maybe an act at a time with notes after. Then the whole play. But hear this: If you want to avoid that "great last run-through before the sets came in and the show went out the window," you had better, during the run-throughs, anticipate all the physical problems of the show. Be sure every entrance, exit, and cross is completed within the floor plan. Use substitute props and furniture in the exact way you'll deal with the real ones. You will then be happy to have the real ones, instead of being disturbed by them. Ap-

Left Page:

To get ready to Spring the trap		To check the "Stage" To get his help To prepare him for the shocker etc. ↓
To act the fool for them		

Right Page: **117**

DIALOGUE: *Hamlet* (Act III, Scene ii)
(Exeunt Rosencrantz and Guildenstern)

Hamlet: What, ho, Horatio!
            (Enter Horatio)

Horatio: Here, sweet lord, at your service.
            (Pull Horatio away from comidor)

Hamlet: Horatio, thou art є'en as just a man
            As e'er my conversation cop'd withal.

Horatio: O, my dear lord. . . .
                              etc.

                              ↓

(Enter King, Queen, Polonius, Ophelia, etc.)

King: How fares our cousin Hamlet?

Hamlet: Excellent, i'faith. . . .
                              etc.

                              ↓

sweet = dear
just = well-balanced
conversation = association
cop'd = dealt

proximate all costume elements that will have any effect on your characterization. It's no good dealing with a corset, let's say, at the dress rehearsal when you've been walking around for three weeks with everything hanging out.

Then come the dress rehearsals and previews with notes given after. Even the reactions of the audience and what they may do to your performance can be anticipated by inviting some friends and relatives (objective ones, if you can find any) to the dress rehearsals.

The rest is, or may be, history.

Emotion

The truth of passion, the verisimilitude of feeling, placed in the given circumstances, that is what our reason demands of a writer or of a dramatic poet.

—Alexander Pushkin

Remember, when suggesting how to make up the left-hand page of your part, the one opposite your dialogue, I promised to tell you what the middle column was for? Well, here goes. It has to do with the touchy subject of emotion.

My continuing hope when I'm directing a play is that I won't ever have to bring up problems of emotion at all: when you talk too much about emotion in acting, it tends to go away. Of the three big motors we use as actors—our mind, our will, and our feeling—the mind is the least capricious. With our mind we make our choices. Our will, which is used in order to execute these choices, is more capricious. Our feeling, the amount and the nature of our emotions, is the most capricious.

There are more misconceptions about emotion—how to work for it, when to work for it, whether to work for it at all —than about any other element of our craft. People seem to think that emotion only implies some huge, general spill of feeling, like crying or terrible anger, whereas actually emotion is something that is always present in one form or another and is sometimes so subtle that it is unidentifiable. You have *some* sort of feeling at all times or you'd be stone dead. There are not just the big ones.

Every imitation "Method" actor loves to cry. Whole acting schools are based on crying: if you can just cry in front of the teacher you're deemed ready for the entire repertoire —from Oedipus to Stanley Kowalski. But, as I said in my *Method—or Madness?* lectures, "If crying were acting, my Aunt Rivka would be Duse."

There's a description of what I'm talking about, the fluidity of emotion as opposed to the one big, solid quality we usually identify in our minds as "emotion," in a review by Bernard Shaw of Duse in Hermann Sudermann's *Magda* in 1895. Shaw tells of Duse's emotional reaction in the scene where, for the first time in many years, she meets the man who had fathered her illegitimate child. The description of the *progress* of her feeling at that point in the play gives us an idea that she was the kind of actress to whom emotion was the result of the things that she thought and experienced— not of her trying for, or pouring on, one solid emotion.

When Duse saw the card that the maid brought announcing the arrival of this man, she wondered how it would be to see him again. When the man entered, she didn't want to look at him because she was afraid to face his eyes. As they sat down and began to have a conversation, she relaxed and took it upon herself to have a little look at him. When she did, she suddenly felt terribly embarrassed and started to blush. That only served to increase her discomfort and finally she simply hid her face in her hands.

What are you going to call the particular emotion in this sequence? There are so many gradations that there is no way in which we can refer to it simply as "shame," or give it any other general name. People who work with such general, cliché titles as "love," "hate," or "anger" become cliché actors.

Let's see if we can define what emotion in acting is, and

how and when to work for it. First, we must distinguish between *emotion* and *emotionalism*. Emotion is that genuine and appropriate feeling that comes from correct art. If the actor understands his character, knows what his inner action is, has established his relationship to the other characters, and has an appropriate reference from his experience going for him, we can assume that any feeling generated by such work will be genuine, true, artistic. Emotionalism is related to pathology in the sense that it is self-induced. If we see it exhibited in life, we say: "Oh, that person is a hysteric, trying to feel something that does not come rationally from living through that particular situation." Unfortunately, when we see that in acting, we don't always say it's pathological. Sometimes we say: "Oh, he's going to get great reviews and leave them cheering every night." Too often, people associate emotionalism with acting.

So, emotion results from correct art, emotionalism from *kvetching*. (On the offchance that there are any gentiles here from places far from New York City, that means constantly complaining or whining or "emoting.")

All actors in history have, at some time or other, had the problem of needing some feeling they were not getting from their rehearsals. Often this occurred when it was necessary for them to come on stage full of some important emotion. They came on "cold," as it were, and thus it was extremely difficult to reach quickly the high pitch of feeling needed, without faking. If they were great, or even good, actors, they felt disinclined to fake. Too many actors have walked out of their dressing rooms, gone to the side of the stage, and then plunged themselves into something they thought was emotion but which was actually a form of energy, only needing *chutzpah* to be turned on and having no relation to the heart or mind. (I don't care how far from New York you come, I'm not going to define *chutzpah* for you. You've got to know *some* theatre terminology.)

In *On Actors and the Art of Acting* George Henry Lewes tells of how the nineteenth-century English actor William Charles Macready was unwilling to come on "cold" at the opening of the third act of *The Merchant of Venice* when Shylock has to be in "a state of intense rage and grief at the flight of his daughter." As preparation, Lewes reports, Macready used to rev up his motor by spending "some minutes behind the scenes, lashing himself into an imaginative rage by cursing *sotto voce* and shaking violently a ladder fixed against the wall." Macready, pre-Stanislavsky, never heard of the "Method," but he knew he needed something to help him make that emotional leap from the calm of his dressing room to the high state of agitation he had to bring on to the stage.

Mrs. Siddons faced a similar problem playing Constance in *King John* at an even earlier date, and hit upon a very different solution. Constance appears in few scenes in the play, but in each one she must function at a fever pitch of emotion. To provide herself with some foundation for this extreme emotion, Mrs. Siddons would stand in the wings from time to time with the young actor who played her doomed son, Arthur, and watch the other characters plotting to take his throne and, eventually, his life. She would "never once, from the beginning of the play to the end of (her) part in it, suffer (her) dressing room door to be closed." Thus she created a continuity and an emotional through-line for herself.

Describing a third kind of pre-"Method" preparation, Ellen Terry tells in her *Memoirs* of visiting Normandy in her twenties: "Long afterwards, when I was feeling as dry as sandpaper on the stage, I had only to recall some of the divine music I had heard in those great churches abroad to become soft, melted, able to act."

Such stories as Terry's have led some actors to confuse *sense* memory with *emotional* memory. Sense memory is the ability to recreate sensory effects without the presence of the actual stimulus: to hear, as Terry did, those cathedral bells without their actually playing, to touch material that is not silk in a way that will make the audience believe it is silk, to pick up a Woolworth glass as if it were fine-stemmed crystal. This ability for sensory recall is sense memory.

It is true, however, that, in working with emotional memory, sensory recall plays a big part, as we'll see shortly when I describe how to use emotional memory. In remembering situations that occurred in the past, the physical aspects of the event—the time of day, the place, the objects, the people—help bring back the emotion. One uses one's sensory recall automatically in emotional memory exercises. But the ability to recreate the truth of objects, sounds, and so on, through our senses and the ability to bring forth *feeling* through emotional memory are two distinct techniques.

The first (and best) source of true and appropriate feeling for an actor is the lines and situations of the play itself. If the actual stuff of the play arouses this natural feeling in the actor, he's home free. It means that he already has in his "storehouse of feelings" some emotional references that automatically relate to the play.

A second way to summon up feeling is through the fullest playing out of strongly chosen, imaginative intentions. Remember in the intention talk I said an actor must choose intentions that will stir him up. You should pick phrases and images in your intentions that will arouse some needed feeling. Rather than say your intention is "to put him down," you could decide "to crush that bedbug." Involved in that image of crushing a bedbug would be a concomitant feeling of disgust. If you've ever crushed one, you know what I'm talking about. An actor should look for intentions that stir up his acting motor. If you choose "to hug her like a baby," that particular, imaginative way of embracing your wife will arouse in you those specific feelings you have about hugging a baby. If you choose simply "to embrace her," the resultant feeling would probably be more general than specific. So strong, colorful, creative choices of intention can lessen the need to work specifically for emotion.

Because people tend to associate emotion with tragedy or "serious" feeling only, let me give an example from comedy. "To tease her" is a possible action. But "to kitzle her," by the very sound of this (made-up) word, implies something funnier and more specific. An actor will feel funnier if he "kitzles" her (and, of course, each actor can make up his own words, words that sound funny to *him*) than if he "teases" her.

BUT suppose, after you've explored all avenues relating to intention, there is still a passage that needs more fullness of feeling than you are mustering, or you have to come on, wracked with emotion, as Nina does in the fourth act of *The Seagull,* without the benefit of a preceding scene to help you gradually build to an emotional peak. At such times an actor must go rummaging around in that storehouse of feelings we spoke of and dredge up something he can use for the particular moment. It is one of the blessings of being an actor, or any kind of artist, that you don't have to cancel out your life. Whatever has happened to you, whether joyous and rewarding or terrible and shameful, is useful material that you can draw on some day in your work.

First, I'm going to illustrate the affective memory exercise we used to do in the Group Theatre days. Then I'm going to explain what I think are the special uses of it and what the possible dangers are. I'll then give you a normal version of the exercise, which you can use with safety in most instances where the very highest state of emotion may not be demanded but where you still need an extra jolt.

The term "affective memory" seems to have derived from the French scientist Theodule Ribot's work *Problèmes de Psychologie Affective* although, as Eric Bentley points out,

Ribot himself used both "emotional memory" and "affective memory" and the terms have become interchangeable. Ribot conducted experiments with human beings and found it was possible to feel the affect of some incident in our past by reliving those events of the past in our imagination. Pavlov, at the same time, had discovered that dogs who had come to associate their eating with the sound of a bell would salivate as soon as they heard the bell, whether or not they were given the food. The dogs would experience the same sensations they had had with the food because they *associated* eating with the sound of the bell.

What actors must always keep in mind is that we don't, we can't, actually remember how we *felt* in some past time. However, if you recall the physical events that happened at some time in your past that then resulted in a strong feeling, the chances are that you will feel something again. Whether that feeling is the same, now that you have lived all these years and are a different person, in a sense, can't be determined or proven—and it doesn't matter. If such an exercise generates an emotion that you can use, you're in business.

Richard Boleslavsky brought Stanislavsky's ideas on affective memory to this country in 1925 and demonstrated them at the American Laboratory Theatre to, among others, Stella Adler, Harold Clurman, Lee Strasberg, and many of the original members of the Group Theatre. From 1931 on, Lee Strasberg taught his version of the technique to the rest of us in the Group. (He's still teaching it.) We overused it to the point of "taking a minute" to prepare emotionally before every single entrance. We'd sit on the side of the stage, eyes closed, relaxed, concentrating, doing some affective memory exercise to "get into the mood" of the upcoming scene. As I remember it, listening for your cue sometimes created a bit of a problem.

To do an authentic affective memory exercise, here's how you proceed: Get into a comfortable position, completely relaxed. Try to recall some event in your past which you think might stir up some feeling usable for the problem in your scene, preferably from your distant past. Emotions derived from recent events are likely to be different in quality or quantity or both when you repeat the exercise. But if you do the exercise based on an experience of some time ago on three different occasions and it works each time, chances are the emotion is in you for good and will always be there, waiting to be summoned.

Suppose you had to get news on stage of a death that was absolutely shattering to you. Nothing in the scene's situation, which, let's say, might be a party, prepares you to receive and react to such news. So you decide to try an affective memory exercise to see if you can find something that will help you in that moment. First, you would search your past for a similar shocking event. Let's say that as a young person you were on the verge of marriage. Your intended was to meet you on the steps of the Public Library on Fifth Avenue and together you would head downtown to get a marriage license. You waited on the library's steps by the lion on the left and, when the appointed time came, your fiancée didn't appear. As time went on you went inside the library, thinking perhaps she was there, you looked at your watch, you looked up and down the street, everyone began to look like her. Finally, you see a friend of yours come down Fifth Avenue and up the steps. The way he's coming toward you up those steps and the expression on his face tell you that it's bad news and it's for you. Your friend announces that your fiancée has been hit by a car and killed.

If you were an actor who had actually had this experience and were called on to play the aforementioned scene of shock, you might decide that this experience from your past was analogous enough to work with. You would then do an emotional memory exercise to see if you still got some usable emotional reaction from the recalling of these events.

Notice that I always refer to remembering *events,* not feelings.

First, as I said before, you would relax yourself physically. If you are muscularly tense in any way, that tends to prevent emotion from flowing. You then try to recall the exact event as it happened back then with all its physical appurtenances, beginning with your arrival on the steps of the library. You can never know what particular physical association might be the one that sets you off. So you would try to recall the look of the lions, the steps, the weather, the people going by, etc., etc. (Here's where sense memory becomes operative.) Try to see again exactly the expression on your friend's face as he approached you. It's quite possible that at any moment now as you're doing this exercise some of the feeling might start to come forth. You might not start feeling something when you recall his words but when you recall his face. It's important to know the exact moment in the event, the button—so to say—that sets you off, your equivalent of Ellen Terry's cathedral bells.

If, by going through this entire recall and repeating it twice more on separate occasions, it works for you each time, then it's usable and in you for good. You may use such an exercise just before you go on stage; it's perfectly easy to do such an exercise in the wings, if necessary, before entering to play your scene. But you can actually get an emotional response *on* the stage at a given moment if you studied what the specific *moment* of the affective memory exercise was that triggered your emotion. Then, when the character in the scene tells you that your mother has died, you would need only that moment of the exercise (the look on your friend's face, let's say) as a substitute to give you the required emotional response. To sum up, you can do the entire exercise as preparation for coming on stage or you can use the "button" during the scene on stage at any time.

When I played a labor spy in Odets's *Waiting for Lefty,*

Elia Kazan acted my brother. In one scene, I was on stage lying to a meeting of taxi drivers and Kazan came out and denounced me as a spy. The head of the union asked him how he could prove I was the spy. "I know because he's my own lousy brother," Kazan answered. At that point I used to blush a deep red every night and run up the aisle and out of the theatre. People used to wonder how I was able to blush every night on cue and assumed it was some sort of trick, that I was holding my breath. It was simple: I had a very strong emotional memory exercise. All I had to do was look at Kazan at that moment and substitute that other person who had once caught me *in flagrante delicto,* as they say in divorce courts, and it worked every single time. It was a transference of that emotional experience onto this stage moment here. It can be done.

Having now told you how, for special, big emotional needs, affective memory exercises can be used either for preparation or in actual scenes, I would like to warn you of certain dangers inherent in the process. I suppose the more subtle technical work is, the more possibility there is of danger lurking. First, in choosing experiences from our own lives, we risk the chance of dredging up personal emotions that may not be apt for the character's feeling at all. They may be very true, but rather reflect the way *you* would feel at that moment rather than the way the character would feel. You have to be very clever to find experiences that serve up the emotions analagous to the character and the situation in the play. The memory exercise I used in *Waiting for Lefty* was so similar to the play's situation that it was an absolutely valid analogy and was therefore usable. It contained all the shame and fright I needed for the moment. But you have to be very careful in your choices. Otherwise you may be feeling truthfully but it may be your *personal* truth, not the *theatrical* truth, not the *character's* truth.

Something like that once happened to Stella Adler in the

Group Theatre days. Stella was far and away our best actress, but this story illustrates how problematical this area of our technique can be, even for an actress of her caliber. In *Big Night* she played a model who, at one point, has to say (I'm paraphrasing), somewhat wistfully, "You may think I'm just a frivolous model, but I actually do love good books and music. However, when I see a gorgeous fur coat in Bergdorf's window I say, *That's* what I really want." It was a wry, humorous line. But Stella delivered the line with genuine sorrow and regret. That was, indeed, a problem Stella had in life, too, and she understood it from her own point of view. She wanted to be a great actress in the Group Theatre and play character roles and be part of an ensemble, but she also wanted to be Lynn Fontanne—and have all the material things Joan Crawford had. The emotion she had in the scene was very "true," but it was Stella's more than the character's. Dawn Powell, the playwright, watched this in rehearsal and said, with admiration and wonder, "Isn't that remarkable? I thought that was a funny line when I wrote it!"

The actor, in other words, might choose something out of his *own* emotional life that is either more or less or different from the responses that would be normal and right for that character in that situation. Stella's feelings about the conflicting desires in her own life were quite different from the character's feelings about a similar conflict. Now considered one of the top acting coaches in the world, she was herself worried about this and other problems arising from the Group's application of the Stanislavsky system, but especially in its use of emotional memory. Stella tracked the Russian director down in Paris and spent six weeks picking his brain. Her return to the Group with clarifications from the horse's mouth was greeted with welcome sighs of relief from the actors.

The next danger is even greater. An actor who uses an affective memory exercise in the wings and wells up with feeling as he comes on stage may hang on to that emotion (it feels so good!) for fear of losing it, instead of playing the scene. His feeling stays on one plane instead of adjusting to the moment-to-moment transitions that result from playing out the scene. It behooves the actor, when he gets on stage, *to play his action,* to release himself from the exercise, so that whatever feeling is there will go up and down according to what transpires in the course of the scene. If you try to "hang on" to your emotion, you will find yourself in what can only be called a "psychological grip." You seem deaf and blind, unable to listen well or see clearly the life around you.

What to do then, to lessen these dangers? First, only use the complete affective memory exercise in cases where no other solution may be possible for you. Then, there is a normal way of working with the idea of affective memory—personal work—that helps an actor to use memories of personal experiences as means of imbuing moments on stage with a desired feeling that may not be as shattering but is needed anyway because all other rehearsal work has not supplied it. It is a form of affective memory that doesn't entail the whole process I have just described.

I've already explained—and it's worth reiterating—that often you have automatic emotional references that supply the proper feeling. Neither sort of exercise is necessary in these instances, and you should not become so obsessed with this whole business of probing into your past that you start to do affective memory exercises of any kind as a habit even when your spontaneous emotional reaction to the situation is strong and *right.*

If I were playing a professor in a university and a character, Richard Nixon maybe, said to me, "College kids are bums," and my reply was, "Don't tell me about college kids," my action might be "to accuse him of a prejudged generalization." I wouldn't need to look for a reference. I have forty years of experience teaching in universities. I was at Yale during Kent State, Vietnam, Cambodia, the Black Panthers, the lot. I saw many kids grow into men before my eyes. Some even got interested in their history ("Was it like this during the McCarthy days?"). So I would have no trouble achieving whatever degree of emotion I needed for that line.

But suppose an occasion arises when, after you've settled on your intention, you feel a certain fullness of emotion is lacking because you *don't* have a specific reference. The audience may believe the *sense* of what you say, but not that you really know what you're talking about specifically from experience. Your line is not coming out of an emotional understanding of the situation.

For example, I have to say to another character, "I like that particular quality in you, Willie." My action is "to realize they don't make them like that any more." Now Willie is not a character with whom I have much to do in the course of the play, nor have we had a close relationship in the past, nor do I have anything to do with him in off-stage action. The sense of that line may be there when I say it, but I don't seem to mean anything specific and important about it. Therefore, in the third act of the play, when someone enters and says, "Willie died this morning," and I'm supposed to be genuinely upset and say, "Oh, not that nice man," I'm going to have trouble with believability—mine and the audience's. My delivery of the line in the first act doesn't help the audience to believe that I really *am* moved by Willie's death. They may understand intellectually that I'm upset because they've been told so, but they have no *sensation* that I genuinely care or cared. Because I, too, only understand the idea of what I'm talking about, without having an emotional reference to give it body.

Here's what I suggest for this kind of problem. Go home or somewhere where you can concentrate. This is the actor's private work, part of his craft, and it needn't be discussed with the director or anyone else. All the director should rightfully have to do is point out the problem. He's not supposed to have to tell the actor how to solve it.

"What can I do?", I ask myself. "What do I mean *specifically* when I say I like that quality about him? *What* quality? What specific trait or traits do *I* understand about him from my experience that will get my emotional juices working truthfully?"

Then I realize that Willie has a kind of innocence. What does that mean to me? Well, for one thing, my father was like that. He used to put a saucer of breadcrumbs for the birds on the kitchen window sill first thing in the morning, every day. He called the birds "chippies." (He also called young girls "chippies.") He used to sleep with a hammer under his pillow in case of burglars in the night. But there would never be any burglars because we didn't have anything to steal. We were too poor. All we had was a hammer. The thought of my father hitting anyone with a hammer anyway was ridiculous. But he had the feeling that he was protecting his family.

Now I know exactly what I'm talking about when I say, "I like that particular quality in you, Willie." I understand that specific kind of innocence. I have found an emotional "reference." I know what I mean in my heart as well as in my head. Now I can never say that line again without that kind of warm feeling springing up. I have an "association."

This is the kind of "normal" affective memory work you can do when you need some emotional help and, if you do, you will find you seldom need to do the other kind except as I have indicated. This seeking out of an emotional reference is sometimes called personalization. You've personalized a moment, made it true to your emotional understanding. Now you can put down, in the middle column of your left-hand page, opposite the line of dialogue in your part, some reminder for yourself (like "Pop").

I don't want to leave this discussion of emotion without pointing out that this work process can be used for any play regardless of style—comedy, tragedy, classical, avant-garde, whatever. It even works in Brecht's plays where our assumption is that the actors "distance" themselves from the characters and simply illustrate the characters' feelings. That is a misunderstanding of the "alienation" effect. If you saw the productions Brecht directed, it was clear that it wasn't what he meant in his essays. Germans love to write essays. But when it came actually to directing his own plays, he did things somewhat differently. He got most of his "epic" points across through production techniques—choruses, signs, and so on. The fine actors of the Berliner Ensemble performed the plays as any good actors perform any plays. They played with complete believability and genuine feeling. What *was* different were the choices they made. They made unsentimental choices. Brecht was against sentimental emotion. He wanted the audience to learn from what went on rather than to be swept away by the actors' personal emotion on stage. When Helene Weigel, selling her wares to survive in the Thirty Years' War, was given a coin in exchange for one of her items in *Mother Courage,* she bit it to see if it was real, not to make Brecht's social point for the audience. Truth is truth in any style.

10

Criticism of Scenes

The technique of acting can never be properly understood without practicing it.

—Michael Chekhov

What follows are comments made after seeing various scenes performed in class. They are in no particular order but together they make up a cross section of the performing problems that arise with the use of the technique in acting actual parts. I've indicated which scene is involved only when it is relevant to my remarks.

One of the problems of thinking actors (like us) is that we sometimes tend to think *before* and *after* the line instead of *on* it. Therefore we get three little bits for the price of one and it's not necessarily three times better. It also slows you down a lot. For example, if you ask me the time and I look at my watch and, realizing I am late for an appointment, answer, "Two o'clock," I must be careful not to

1. Stare at my watch in disbelief, shake it a bit, hold it to my ear to see if it's ticking, look at it again, then,

2. Mumble, "Two o'clock," as if that information is completely unimportant, and then,

3. Gasp, realizing I am late, and dash off.

That's three scenes, the first and the third being alive and the second one, where the dialogue is spoken, dead. If I accomplished 1 and 3 (staring at my watch in disbelief because I realize I'm late) *as* I cried, "Two o'clock!", all that juicy performing would vibrate through the words and the text would profit, instead of its being a mere appendage to the acting.

* * *

Be careful, in speaking verse, especially a well-known passage like this Hamlet monologue, not to give the impression that you know it. Richard Burton was shaken up during a monologue he was speaking at one *Hamlet* performance because Winston Churchill, sitting in the front row, repeated the words along with him in those famous Churchillian accents, proving that *he* knew it, too. Without slowing down, and without disturbing the inner rhythm, you can occasionally take that infinitesimal second to "look for" a word (or a phrase) which will keep the sense of spontaneity going. This is especially true of any "literary" word that might suspiciously sound more like the author talking than the character. This tiny "stroke" before you "find" the word takes that curse off it.

* * *

After the final Nina-Treplev scene from *The Seagull* by Anton Chekhov:

Don't try to cry. If anything, try *not* to cry. Certainly not on cue. You aren't a faucet. That is not to say Nina isn't crying in this scene. But don't ever push a button saying, "Here's where I must cry because she just said she 'hasn't cried for two years.'" You must do all the work that will lead you to the proper feeling. Know what you're doing there. Know exactly what's gone before, not only in those two years, but in the moments just before you came on. Find your emotional references for the situation you are in. Do your preparation. When you enter, deal with Treplev. Deal with the fact that Trigorin is probably in the house. That's all you've got to do. It's plenty, without worrying about "turning on" any feeling. If you're working right, in your situation, the proper emotion will be there. If not, we examine the work. But don't fool around with the problem of "feeling" or it will either go away altogether or just be simulated. Finally, no matter how hysterical your feeling may get, *keep talking.* In other words, play the action, not the emotion. You will then avoid the "psychological grip" you found yourself in.

After the drinking scene from *Fallen Angels* by Noël Coward:

I know it's hard to avoid camping in this kind of comedy. But if you don't, it has the same effect on us as "playing the characterization" instead of the intentions. We see the "comic approach" instead of the scenes. The remedy is to be sure to justify all your character elements with inner choices that will fill them with truth, albeit comic truth. This will keep you busy with your intentions and unaware of your comic effects. Your comedy will result from the playing of these comically chosen intentions. The more you believe in those choices, then, the funnier the scene will be.

(I remember telling Henry Winkler at the Yale Drama School, "Don't *try* to be funny all the time. Play the scene. If it's a funny scene, it will be funny." After his million-dollar success as the Fonz on TV, he returned to visit the school. I said to him, "You see, Henry, if you had only listened to me, you'd have been a pauper today.")

Finally, when the fight in the scene reaches its climax, remember not to abandon your sense of physical ease for strain. (The characters' being "loaded" helps here, too.) Muscular tension is not the same thing as intensity.

What it wouldn't hurt actors to have, in addition to that precious sense of truth we all cling to, is some awareness of dynamics. You may say that's the director's province and, of course, it is; but if performing in a play is an artistic act, based on a sense of truth, but *designed,* then it behooves actors to pay as much attention to dynamics as musicians or painters do. An all-slow or all-fast symphony, unrelieved by any changes in tempo, is unlikely. An Ad Reinhardt all-black painting has, at least, a couple of shades of black in it.

Now I don't mean that, for variety, you arbitrarily go faster or slower, or louder or softer. I do mean that if you are aware of the need for some dynamic change, you can always find the inner justification, in terms of intention, to accomplish it.

Another point about form: the sections of your scene were well realized but we felt where the "seams" were. Each section was accomplished and then the next started. Do it once more and try to bring it all together in a continuous flow. Then, if you ever do actually want to end something abruptly and make the start of the next section sharp, that will, in itself, be dynamic.

* * *

One of the dangers of scene classes is that we try to crowd the material of the whole part into the one scene we're doing. Although it's important for you to understand the entire play to be able to act your chosen scene, be careful that you just reveal the material needed in the particular section you're doing. All facets of a character aren't operating all the time throughout a play, although the temptation is there to get them all going while we're playing our one part of the piece. Avoid that tendency like the plague.

* * *

How shall I say this? Well, let me tell you first the effect you created. It was good, but effortful. We saw you "making it." We noticed the wheels turning, even though they turned in the right direction. We want to see *past* your acting effects to the play itself. Advice? If I said, "Don't you play the part, let the part play you," would it help? I mean that once you have mastered what you wish to accomplish moment by moment, give in to it, surrender to it, believe in it, let it happen.

Less than one hundred percent of what you're working for, without effort, is better than one hundred percent achieved with a strain that we notice.

* * *

After the Act II, Scene ii, monologue from *Hamlet:*

The particularizing of the meaning of a word: that's what I wish to address. We know that by the process of intention we arrive, not just at the sense of a line or a speech, but at that sense plus what we wish to convey with the dialogue. So, too, individual words (or phrases) are not there just for definition but for what is implied by our use of them. For example, you, Hamlet, when you said, "This *player* here," seemed merely to be identifying him. Actually, you are making the point that an *actor* could have tears in his eyes for a character, Hecuba, and that you, Hamlet, have not yet been moved to avenge your father's murder. So, you see, that word "player" has to be invested with that particular meaning. You must dig for what you mean *specifically,* not only by the speeches and lines, but by the very individual words themselves.

* * *

After the Act II Garden scene from *The Importance of Being Earnest:*

There's a canard abroad that the actor shouldn't know when a line is meant by the author to be funny. If you're talking about a character who doesn't mean to be funny but is, that's one thing. If you're talking about not *trying* to be funny, but accomplishing the tasks in the scene truthfully with choices that are funny, that's another thing. But, if you're talking about the seeming innocence both you actresses had that there was a particle of wit in Oscar Wilde's lines, forget it. You were so unaware of the humorous gold in the dialogue that it escaped us too. It doesn't hurt to know, for example, that Gwendolen, when discovering through her lorgnette how young and pretty Cecily is, says, "You are here on a short visit, I suppose," that she is not just inquiring about the length of her stay in the country. Back to the drawing board, ladies.

* * *

After a scene from *Orpheus Descending:*

You're too "poetic"—your character, Val, doesn't know he's been written by Tennessee Williams.

11

More Helpful Hints

> While everyone understands that it is a primary requisite in a singer that he should not only have a voice, but know how to *sing,* very few seem to suspect that it is not less a primary requisite in an actor that he should know how to *speak.*
>
> —George Henry Lewes

Articulation

I find, in rehearsing with actors for actual productions, a recurrent problem that, in a way, is a result of work we do to eliminate other problems. It is the lack of proper articulation of the text. The hope is that the actors have true feeling. We also hope the actors have specific, original, theatrical characterizations. And we hope the actors are going to play with intention and not just give "line readings." With all of that accomplished, these well-trained performers, who know that acting is more than clear speech, standing up straight, and not bumping into furniture, still have to face the following: Not always does all their good rehearsal work go back into *feeding the dialogue.* It does not always serve the moment-to-moment expression of the *words* that are the inspiration of the interpretation arrived at. After all, you got the characterization, the intentions, etc., from the suggestions in the dialogue.

What can happen is one of these disasters:

The actor "plays the mood." His feeling is true and strong, but "washes over" the dialogue. We sense his emotion is felt truthfully and we get a general *sense* of believability but not the specific point emerging from the dialogue and triggering that emotion. Poor articulation. (I'm not talking now about the results of the psychological grip I referred to in discussing emotion. The actor may be "playing a mood" that is altogether appropriate and he may alter that mood in the proper way at the proper time. But still he is not articulating.)

Second, the actor "plays the characterization." We believe he's ancient or stammering or military or "mittel-European," but the words, phrases, sentences that demonstrate those character elements are swept away in the clever expression of his characterization. (Playing the characterization at the expense of articulation is not the same as playing the characterization at the expense of intention. It's the former problem I'm addressing myself to now, a problem that can arise even when character elements have not distracted the actor from playing with intention.)

Finally, the actual intention does not seem to have worked itself back into the dialogue. We know she's "tearing the top of her husband's head off" with fine fury, but we sense that the words are needed only for the sound of the fury and that gibberish could have served as well. The shafts aimed at the husband do not light up the specific language in the script. Intention without understanding words is no better than understanding words without intention.

So, the acting is clear, but the dialogue is not. Take the corniest example: Someone says to you, "Who was that lady I saw you with last night?" You say, "That was no lady, that was my wife." The "truth" of that joke lies not only in your righteous indignation but in your juxtaposition, with clear articulation, of the word "lady" with the word "wife." If you don't juxtapose, there is no joke. In other words, if you are so true to yourself and to your emotion that you say the line without clearly bringing out those two words, nobody is going to laugh. They'll only know you're being truthful. They'll know you're denying what the other guy said to you, that you're contradicting him with fine feeling. But you have not taken that contradiction and poured it back into the style of the dialogue that gave you the idea of the *way* you were contradicting him. You may choose the correct intention, "to describe your wife as a monstrosity," but that's still not the whole joke, the essence of which is the way the words are laid out. If you play the mood and the characterization and the intention and don't relocate them all into their source in the text, you have not completed your work on that moment.

I have, on occasion, sat watching actors I'd carefully rehearsed and found myself thinking, "What was that they *said?* I don't understand what they said." I see the acting and it looks good. (After all, I helped them with it.) They have good characterization and thinking and feeling. The only thing we don't get is what they are *saying.* But we don't want to admire the acting at the expense of the dialogue. You have to be very careful that you build the dialogue up with all your work on the subtext, the characterization, the emotion. And each time you work on one of these elements, use it to make the words that much clearer, not that much vaguer.

Why go to class?

Aside from the obvious reasons why actors study—to consolidate their technique or to learn how to work on a part —there is one other important objective to be pursued in class: to dig out and tackle any areas of weakness in your craft. Whether it's poor concentration, resistance to characterizing, or any one of a hundred hang-ups you might have, latch on to it the moment it shows up in an exercise or a scene in class and grapple with it till it's conquered. Don't rationalize your weaknesses—cure them. As a kid, when I studied the cello, I discovered the forefinger on my left (fingering) hand had a slight bend in it that made notes played with that finger go sharp. I couldn't say, "Tough luck. I've got a lot of other good notes." I had to embark on an endless stretching exercise for the poor finger that went on all day, every day, until the finger got into place. It made for some hairy moments going to class on the subway, with what would look like a beckoning forefinger.

A classic example of resistance overcome and mission accomplished involved the young Marlon Brando. He was in that remarkable class in 1947 that I was privileged to teach in the first year of the Actors Studio. Elia Kazan, who was one of the founders with me, decided to teach the newer actors, and I took those with more experience. Since my group contained such worthies, in addition to Marlon, as Monty Clift, Mildred Dunnock, Maureen Stapleton, and a couple of dozen more of similar stature, there was no question of "teaching them to act." They knew how. But I tried to seek out whatever area of resistance any of them might have had and make them face it.

To Marlon I said, "I'm going to pick a scene for you, from a high comedy, where you play some sort of elegant royalty." I settled on Robert Sherwood's *Reunion in Vienna,* with Marlon as the Archduke Rudolf Maximilian of the House of Habsburg. Marlon winced. I pressed on. "I want the works: uniform, sword, cigarette holder, waltz music off stage, Habsburg lip, the lot." Each time I asked if the scene was ready, Marlon had an excuse—"I forgot the phonograph record," or something. Finally I said, "Look, why go to class at all if not to stretch yourself? Even if you never play a part like that, it will at least help you find the prince in any bum you might have to do. Don't hang around in comfortable places." Finally the great day came. As the lights came up, Marlon slowly circled his quarry, the beautiful Elena, and, with that unpredictability we were to get to know so well, he slapped her, grabbed her, kissed her savagely and, with an impeccable Habsburg accent, murmured softly: "How long has it been since you were kissed like that?" The first laugh acted like a blood transfusion on Marlon, and from then on through the scene he proved he could also be as fine a light comedian as the young John Barrymore if he wanted to.

How to audition

No good actor *likes* to audition. Some of our best, like Maureen Stapleton, simply can't. They'd rather not have the part than be put up on trial. I once asked the late Jimmy Dean to read Sakini's opening monologue in *The Teahouse of the August Moon* for the author and producer because I knew he'd be a fine replacement for the David Wayne part in the touring company. After much persuasion, he got as far as the center of the Martin Beck stage, opened his mouth, and fell to the floor in a fit of hysterical giggling. I propelled him into a dressing room and assured him it was not his talent that was on trial. As a director, I had sold the powers-that-be on that. We simply wanted to know if he could manage the Oriental accent he'd been practicing. "It's just a technical point, and an important one," I said. "If Laurence Olivier were required to do a tap dance in a part, not only would the director and author want to be sure he could do it, *he'd* want to know, too." Out Jimmy went again and collapsed again. I'll never know how much was excessive shyness and how much lack of technique.

Well, then, if you can bring yourself to believe it's your fitness for the job that's being examined and not your psyche, what should you do? First, try in every way you can to find out who may be out in that auditorium and what they might possibly be looking for. Ask the stage manager, your agent, the other actors coming off the stage, anyone, for hints, especially if you've just been handed a tiny audition scene and you haven't read the whole play. (Of course, if complete scripts have been made available, the value of reading the entire play is enormous.) Finally, when you get out there, if there's still something crucial you must know, take the chance of asking those menacing faces out there, "Does this girl really mean it when she praises this guy?" or, "Is this character supposed to be drunk here?" I, for one, am always happy someone is interested enough to ask.

If it's a general audition, let's say for a regional theatre, investigate the repertory and the style of acting they may be looking for. Choose material that is varied, even if it's just two two-minute monologues—a serious classical piece and a funny modern one, for example. Also material that will show not only your range but your best qualities. When a singer picks a song with which to audition, he tries to find one that shows off his best high and low, loud and soft, tones, not just one color.

Always use good energy. Not being able to hear you well scares the hell out of that audience—especially the playwrights.

If it's a scene you're reading, even with a mumbling stage manager, *talk* and *listen.* I can't tell you how impressive that can be if you really do it. It makes you look as if you know your business. It will even wake the stage manager up to better cooperation than if you ignore him because you're not "getting" enough from him.

If it's a monologue you're doing, ask them if they'd mind your using one of them out there as a partner in case you'd like to connect with someone. (Choose a producer or an agent if you can. It leaves the director or the author free to judge you—or make notes.) If you don't succeed in this, you can use other partners—your own self, God, the world, an imaginary person or crowd, etc. Choosing someone, or something, to lay it on roots you in a "scene" and tends to keep you from "reciting."

Don't be resistant if the director, who may be wary of an effective but glib audition, asks you to improvise something —or to do your scene over in a new way he suggests. It will not only show you can take direction, but will be a proof of your versatility.

If you don't get the part, try not to abandon all hope. Aside from the possibility that they might just be dumb, other factors may be present you should think about. It may not be your acting at all that was in doubt. It may have been some essential quality of personality you seemed to have that would have given the wrong impression for the particular character being cast. I was down to the last two candidates for the lead in Agatha Christie's murder mystery *Witness for the Prosecution,* and I chose the one that I knew had slightly less pure acting talent than the other because the other had a kind of mature, knowing aspect that might just make the audience guess he "did it." The one I chose had an incontrovertible innocence that could fool the audience until the "triple whammy" at the end, when we discover the dear boy was indeed responsible for bashing the rich old lady's skull in, as well as a few other unpleasant things. That, of course, was the fun of it all and what had to be kept in mind when casting.

Marking

What should an actor do during a "starting and stopping" rehearsal when the director has to check the lights, the sound cues, or solve some other technical problem? Play with minimal energy, of course, not "full out," to save yourself. This is called "marking it." But there are good and bad ways of marking.

When a singer marks in order to save his voice, he can either use *mezza voce* (half the usual volume) or sing an octave lower to relieve strain on his voice. A ballerina, arriving at her thirty-two *fouettés* in a long rehearsal, might stand there and whip her hand around thirty-two times to mark what the feet should be doing, and then end up in the finishing position. But here's the point: the singer "hears" in his inner ear not only the correct notes but the correct dynamics, too. He just cuts down the size. So, too, the ballerina experiences in her kinesthetic "sense memory" the correct steps, the correct attitude of the body, etc., even though she's saving her energy.

What is the corresponding process for actors? You can cut down on your emotion and your vocal energy but, on pain of death, don't fail to keep your thinking, your inner line, going. That is what holds our form together. It is dangerous to mark by simply gabbling or mumbling. You are rehearsing a non-scene then, and when you get back to playing it with full energy, your thinking may have become muddled. Correct talking and listening, even on a low level of energy, gives you more rehearsals preserving the shape of your scenes. That's the only safe way to mark in acting.

Perils of scene classes

The most prevalent problem arising out of scene classes is low energy and, subsequently, inaudibility. Instead of stage energy, you use room energy—I suppose because you're in a room. But if you sang *piano* when *forte* was required in an aria and waited till you got to the operatic stage before unleashing your volume, you'd be in big trouble. Watch that. Don't be "classroom actors."

Another danger comes from the fact that we choose scenes to work on that are climactic, "high" scenes. We certainly don't want to spend good class time on that expository bit where you come in, hang up your hat, and ask how everyone is. You want to work on some confrontation scene with a good bit of conflict in it. What can happen then, if you've spent all your studying time with big moments, is that the necessary small moments where you *do* have to just hang up your hat and ask how everyone is are apt to be filled with mysterious "meaning." Everything gets to be significant and so nothing is. This is a common fault of thinking actors. Pray you, avoid it.

Spontaneity

Actors sometimes wonder if a loss of spontaneity might not ensue through the knowledge of the subtext. It certainly might if, when you're out there acting, you were thinking, "Now what's my objective here?" That's playing your technique instead of the play. It is hoped that all the designing of the inner line, indeed all your choices, should be absorbed and gracefully "forgotten" as you have your run-throughs of the play. They become inextricably bound up in the dialogue, unconsciously part of your behavior. All you need to know when you go out there on the stage, the only order you need give yourself, is to "locate" yourself in the play. If this is the scene where you decide to break off with your husband forever, that's all you need to know. When you come on, you must be sure to talk and listen (always), and then the way that talking and listening forms itself into its sections is automatic *because* you have worked it out and rehearsed it. But you are free to "have it happen," to experience it yourself as if for the first time, and so preserve that precious sense of spontaneity we all want. You might say that instead of your playing the play, the play plays you.

Dealing with your partner

How many times have I heard an actor ask, "What do I do if my partner doesn't give me what I need?" Well, we've already talked about how Maria Ouspenskaya solved,

through justification, what could have been an impasse between her and her director. The same ability to justify can
get you out of partner trouble, too.

Suppose, for an obvious example, you have to say to a
completely dry-eyed actress, "Don't cry, sweetheart." You
don't have to feel like a fool. Look for a justifiable way of
solving the problem. For example: to stop her in case she's
about to cry. Incorporate what seems to be missing in your
partner's contribution into your own intention. It may very
well even improve your work. Otherwise, *you* may seem to
be the one who's false.

The greatest instance of this capitalizing on what could
have been an impossible situation was the remarkable performance of Shaw's *Candida* by Laurette Taylor in the thirties. It was a week's stock engagement at the Playhouse in
Mt. Kisco. I started out, in a rickety "Flivver," early every
afternoon to allow for daily breakdowns along the way. I was
in my seat for the opening curtain every night that unforgettable week. Realizing that each of the men in the play, Morell
and Marchbanks, is a child in one way or another, the choice
between them might not be too interesting. What she, as
Candida, wanted to feel were the strengths in each, so that
in the end, forced to choose, she would be minus one of the
two ingredients that would, for her, make up a complete man
—the adventurous poet and the solid provider.

Those worthy qualities, however, were not to be found
in the performances of the two actors, and so Laurette set
about providing those virtues *for* them. If her husband
seemed a hearty child and nothing else, she'd look at him as
if to say, "I know there's more to you than that. Why cover
it over?" When Marchbanks leaped about in the prescribed
manner of stage poets, she'd think, "Underneath all that
adolescent behavior is the real strength of the poet." When
she sat them both down at the end of the play to make her
choice, she took a long look at each of them, summing up all

the elements of their characters, realized and unrealized, in their performances. She chose Morell because he needed her the most, but we had no sense of the usual happy ending with husband and wife reunited. What we saw was a woman knowing that with the poet's exit, the dream of adventure was going out the door and out of her life forever.

This was the work of a great artist enhancing her performance by living in the truth of her surroundings and not complaining of not being "given" what she needed.

How to listen to criticism

First of all, don't take criticism levelled at others as necessarily applying to you, too. Too many times I have noticed that when I say to someone on one side of the room, "Relax, relax, you're too tense," the guy on the other side, lolling sleepily in his chair, hears that and happily slumps practically to the floor. "Not you," I yell, "you tense up!" What you should do, when listening to others being criticized, is relate what is being said to what you saw performed. In that way, you might understand something of the technique that you can apply to yourself in your own way at some time.

Next: criticism directed at you. Unless the director or teacher is an idiot (in which case, get out fast), try not to listen too defensively. I know it's hard because we tend to take the remarks as referring to us personally—our legitimacy or our talent—rather than to the problem—technical, interpretive, whatever. Even if the criticism falls short of a correct analysis of what happened, the fact that the director or teacher feels *something* is awry should interest you enough to try to trace the source of the trouble. Sometimes, you might find that something you did earlier is not clear enough and *that's* what is making this particular moment seem wrong. After all, if the person sitting out there got an impression, it behooves you to examine your work for the source of that impression.

Then, too, study the critical remarks in relation, not only to your own part, but as they might refer to the whole scene, or the whole play. All this speculation will help you to feel, as you make your corrections, that you are not just "doing what the man said," but are dealing with your mistakes and improvements with the same sense of the whole with which you approached your original choices.

As an aside, I'd like to clear up what some actors might feel is an unfair variance in tone as a teacher or a director gives criticism to this or that actor or actress. It is perfectly true that sometimes there is a degree of toughness in the way a performer is criticized. Other times, the director can be inexplicably gentle with someone who's obviously gotten something wrong. The reason is not (or should not be) partiality. Rather, there are some actors who, at a certain point in the rehearsal, or in their career, for that matter, need to be shook up. Others occasionally need to be encouraged, to be given confidence. So the director, too, with judgment, often needs to consider not only "what" he is saying and "why" he is saying it, but "how."

During the run

Never forget that after the play opens another director enters the picture—the audience. If you let them, they can pull this or that moment out of shape to the detriment of a scene as a whole. Sometimes they can illuminate something you or the director missed and you can adjust to that. More often they are laying booby traps. For example, you might get a laugh where you never expected it. You now "go for" that laugh. There are dangers in that, not the least of which is that you might lose the laugh altogether. What they are laughing at may be something in your situation that was set up before. If you alter your thinking to conform to the audience reaction, you may kill what was making it funny in the first place. Your character's ignorance of the humor in the situation may have been the heart of the humor.

During the run of a play the audience can sometimes, with their restlessness, tell you that what was once the point of a scene may have been altered or watered down through repetition. You will be glad then that you have your "score," your part with all the original intentions carefully noted. By going over it, you may find that in this or that spot you are no longer executing your proper objective. Or worse, you may have changed it altogether. The audience, or your partner, may have pulled you away from your original inner action. You can now restore it.

Finally, an understudy going on, or a replacement, requires a reexamination of your subtext so that it may, without fundamentally altering the play's meaning, be adjusted to the new actor.

I was witness to a remarkable instance of this adjusting when the late Franchot Tone quit, during the run of the Group Theatre's *Success Story* by John Howard Lawson, to go to Hollywood. Franchot had played the boss of a business that was slowly taken over by an employee, Luther Adler. Stella Adler played the secretary of the firm and, although deeply in love with Luther's character, kept up a charming, innocent flirtation with Franchot, simply because he was such a handsome boss to take dictation from. For some reason, Stella hadn't had a chance to go through the play with Roman Bohnen, Franchot's replacement. I was standing in the wings as Stella came on in her first scene with the new boss, stenographer's pad and pencil poised delightfully and the usual happy, slightly teasing smile on her face. With one look at the aging, sober-faced Bohnen, I saw Stella drop her entire sexy manner to the floor like a cape. I'm sure she missed it, but she was an artist and couldn't retain what would have been an untruthful relationship with this new partner.

12

An Actor Transforms

Ceremonies are the outward expression of inward feeling.

—Lao-Tze

"It was like watching an accident," actress Helen Westley said in the thirties, trying to describe the impact of the Group Theatre's naturalistic style of acting. This true-to-life ensemble playing, compared by Brooks Atkinson to the Moscow Art Theatre, had a lasting influence on acting here and abroad. (The Group invaded the London theatre in 1938 with Odets's *Golden Boy.*) In the late fifties, with the emergence of the Living Theatre, the next important avant-garde plateau was reached. Everyone was obliged to take a fresh look at the American acting style and the training methods for actors.

As the economic noose tightened around Broadway's neck, the number of serious new plays originating in the commercial theatre reduced considerably. Off-Broadway became the haven, not only for the Living Theatre, but for most of the new playwrights and directors. Soon mounting costs began to threaten small theatres as well as large. Strangely enough, however, as the audience for serious new plays (and musicals) seemed to shrivel (I say "seemed" because maybe it was the plays that were shrivelling), theatre in "the provinces" began to blossom. Decentralization set in, with re-

153

gional and university theatres popping up all over the country, Tyrone Guthrie's in Minneapolis being one of the first.

Then, too, playwrighting styles were altering. Instead of good and bad "well-made" plays, we had good and bad "fragmented" plays—fragmented as in the "break-up" of form of the Cubist painters.

Professional actors, finding work scarce—unless they were doing voice-overs on TV commercials or working as digestives in dinner theatres—packed their bags and headed off to San Francisco, Minneapolis, Houston, or Washington. There they were slapped with a repertory of plays in all styles, classical and avant-garde, light years away from the daily behavior patterns they had previously based their acting on.

New scripts being too scarce to sustain year-round companies, actors found themselves faced with characters in plays of all styles and periods, from a Renaissance prince to a Munchkin—and, in some plays, a Renaissance prince in Scene i and a Munchkin in Scene ii. They not only had to "use" themselves, they had to *transform* themselves. The dialogue no longer hit them where they lived as in "Attention must be paid" or "I have always depended on the kindness of strangers." Instead, the text might go something more like this, from the beginning of Aeschylus' *Agamemnon:*

> I ask the gods some respite from the wariness/of this watch-time measured by years I lie awake/elbowed upon the Atreidae's roof dogwise to mark/the grand processionals of all the stars of night/burdened with winter and again with heat for men,/dynasties in their shining blazoned on the air,/these stars, upon their wane and when the rest arise.

The next week they were handed Lucky in *Waiting for Godot* and this is what they had to wrap around their tongues:

> Given the existence as uttered forth in the public works of
> Puncher and Wattmann of a personal God quaquaquaqua with
> white beard quaquaquaqua outside time without extension
> who from the heights of divine apathia divine athambia. . . .

Try *that* on your old Stanislavsky.

The problem was this: How do you apply your ability to
play through the situation—that basic technique of talking
and listening with intention, experiencing the truth of the
moment, handed down from the Group Theatre, and at
which the American actors were, and are, the best in the
world—to the new writing or, for that matter, to the problem
of verse in classics? And how do you add to your appreciation
of the rhythm and music of Macbeth's "Tomorrow and tomorrow and tomorrow . . ." the inner underpinnings of the
knowledge that his wife has just died and not lose the properties of the verse?

Now, it's true that many "conceptual" productions of
classics encouraged the avoidance of the problems of choral
speech, verse, period, etc., by simply shifting (in the name of
"modernizing") the time and place of the action from then-
and-there closer to here-and-now. Mind you, I'm not opting
for museum-like faithfulness to classics. A play is written to
be interpreted on the stage, not to be read in the library. As
new ideas in staging and writing develop, new ways to pro-
duce plays are mandated. I'm not denigrating imaginative
concepts or vital, new approaches to the playwright's intention. "Conceptual" directing was not just invented; directors
have always had their personal visions of plays they were
directing. No good artist works without some concept, considered or intuitive, whether he writes an article in *The
Drama Review* about it or not. And the fact that he can write
the article is no guarantee that he can execute his concept
with artistry on stage.

What I object to is the deliberate vulgarization of a text
and the author's intention in the name of concept. We don't

really need a *King Lear: Superstar* or *The Three Chicano Sisters*. This dilution of the true meaning of avant garde has taken its toll on the experimental theatre movement. Too much is vanity. This *arrière-garde* attitude has hastened a return to conservatism in the theatre.

One of the most beautifully "conceived" productions of a classic I ever saw was Roger Planchon's direction of *Georges Dandin*. Instead of either looking at the traditional way of playing Molière on the stage *or* trying to "modernize" or update the material in some way, Planchon simply approached the text as though it were an unknown script handed him. He then studied the *life* of those times and, for the first time, we saw peasants and aristocrats as they must have really been, not as they've come down to us through the Comédie Française or any other theatre. It was really like seeing Molière for the first time and was, therefore, a genuinely refreshing experience.

For an organic approach to style, I take my cue from Thomas Carlyle:

> It is meritorious to insist on forms. Religion and all else naturally clothes itself in forms. All substances clothe themselves in forms. But there are suitable true forms, and then there are untrue, unsuitable. As the briefest definition one might say, Forms which *grow* round a substance, if we rightly understand that, will correspond to the real Nature and purport of it, will be true, good; forms which are consciously *put* round a substance, bad. I invite you to reflect on this. It distinguishes true from false in Ceremonial Form, earnest solemnity from empty pageant, in all human things.

When Treplev realizes in the last act of *The Seagull* that, in writing, it's not a question of old forms or new forms, he might have added that it's also not a question of form for its own sake, devoid of its source in the content. This is an old polemic, of course, but how often it is forgotten in our mounting of plays, especially classics, and in our criticism of the productions.

I suspect a good many smart-aleck side-steppings of the problems of style in a script have to do not so much with originality, but with an inability to deal with the problems. It's like deciding to be an abstract painter because you can't draw. If you view a retrospective exhibition of Mondrian's paintings, you see how his later distillations in the form of squares and oblongs evolved from his gradual elimination of the inessentials of nature, which he *had* realized in his earlier work. Likewise, Samuel Beckett's "style" of playwrighting is not arbitrarily assumed, but results from the reduction of life and language to the simplest eloquence.

I once heard Arnold Schoenberg yell: "I don't write *twelve tone* compositions. I write twelve tone *compositions!*" Another famous musician, Artur Schnabel, was approached by a woman with the question, "Are you one of that school of pianists who believe in playing in time, or do you believe in playing with feeling?" Schnabel replied, for all of us, "Madame, what is to prevent me from feeling in time?"

When faced with the problem of stretching himself to include the world repertory in addition to Clifford Odets's kitchens, the first thing the serious American actor did was "go to class." Everywhere, people were studying voice, diction, movement, fencing, Yoga, Judo, T'ai Chi, to mention only a few. (It's interesting that, while we threw ourselves into solving the problems of style over here, Peter Brook, a stylish English director, was at the same time trying to get some truthful subtext into his *King Lear* rehearsals through improvisation. The daily rehearsal log shows that the younger actors complied at once while some of the older ones rebelled. Their Shakespearean battle cry, as usual, was, "It's all in the words, love.") If an actor was lucky enough to track down the few good teachers in each discipline, it is quite possible that he might have expanded the range and volume of his voice. He might have cleared up some speech defects and he might have freed his restrictive body in a good movement class.

For all those classes, what happened was this. There seldom was a perfect marriage, throughout a company, of the form of the piece—the feel of the language, the accents, the verse rhythms, the easy assumption of the physical behavior of the period or the class of the parts—with the full, dynamic playing out of the truthful insides of the characters.

Those who could accomplish the form, the "outside," so to say, often faked the inside. Those who could play the inner truth as well as they did in their realistic roles were apt to ignore, or mangle, the poetic aspects of the language. *They didn't understand that, for "total" acting, the inside and the outside must both be realized: that, indeed, each is derived from the other.*

The newly trained actor might have a fine appreciation of the lyricism in Orsino's opening speech in *Twelfth Night* and he may now have the vocal technique to perform that speech. Except, of course, that his rendition might lapse into the affected "mooniness" we've mentioned that so many actors are prone to when confronted with beautiful poetry.

And what happens when he is playing Hamlet and comes to the scene with his mother, following the performance of "The Murder of Gonzago"? Our good, truthful actor is now full up with emotion, piled on from these preceding, momentous events: (1) the exultation from the King's guilty reaction to the play, (2) his realization of the perfidy of his friends, Rosencrantz and Guildenstern, (3) nearly killing the King at prayer and, now, (4) actually killing Polonius, while trying to shame his mother.

I can think of some actors who could break your heart with the fullness of feeling the scene demands, but not too many who could experience that same degree of emotion without in some way mangling the language.

How then can we apply, and not abandon, our inner technique to parts presenting definite problems of style? I invite you to consider a two-pronged attack: a reexamination of our training methods and a careful scrutiny of rehearsal procedure.

The results obtained in the voice and movement classes (either private or in universities and acting schools) are often satisfactory in those classrooms or in scenes fairly relaxed so that the control of voice, speech, and movement is accomplished easily. But, when faced with a problem of high emotion or very special period movement, the gains of all those fine lessons fly out the window. The actor reverts to his old patterns or, conversely, if he's conscious of his voice or body, inhibits the full expression of his insides. I have heard actors, when confronted with the news that the emotion was great but we couldn't understand half the words, wail, "What am I to do? Think of my acting or my speech?" "Neither," I say. "When you're acting, you only think of what point you're trying to make in your situation. Technical problems of speech, voice, movement—*and* emotion—should be behind you, should be second nature by now." If, in our training, and if, in our rehearsing, we have always asked ourselves not only: *"What* am I doing and *why* am I doing it?" but: *"How* am I doing it?", we wouldn't get into this trouble later on.

When I was chairman of the Acting and Directing Departments at the Yale School of Drama and could control scheduling, I arranged that once every week a long period was set aside for a workshop session conducted by the acting, voice/speech, and movement teachers. Naturally, during the week there were technique exercises, warm-ups, drills of all kinds, etc., that each discipline had to do separately. But we also had this one extended period when all three departments were in the same room together. The point was to ensure that the means of expression, vocal and physical, *adhered* to even the wildest display of feeling, and that truthful acting could thrive in the face of even the most rigid vocal and physical demands of an unfamiliar style.

Suppose we had an actor working on the Act IV, Scene

i, monologue from *Timon of Athens,* as we did one day. Timon is outside the walls of the city and is hurling lightning bolts of venomous curses back to the loathsome parasites of his now-hated Athens, which he is fleeing forever. The talented actor's rage was stupendous. But it worried me that, if he had to play the part through, he'd never make it. I turned to the voice teacher. "What do you think?" She immediately went to work for a good little while, suggesting this and that, in an attempt to open his throat, with promises to do more with him in her voice class during the week. "Now," I said, "armed with this relief of proper vocal production, start from the top. But, whatever happens, you perform your acting tasks exactly as you did the first time. Let whatever results you got from the voice work you just did *be* there in whatever degree they might occur. Don't *you* think of your voice production, though." Well, the vocal improvement was marked, if not total, with the inside motor still functioning in the same high gear. And the results—much more to be desired than might have been achieved if the actor had gone off to a voice and speech teacher, got his sound and diction up to snuff and, in the process, lost some of the precious freedom of creating the truth of the situation and the size of the emotional outpouring he was so eminently capable of.

We followed the identical routine with problems of movement: the stance and walk resulting from the costume of an Elizabethan man or a Restoration fop, the balancing of an Edwardian hat on the top of a lady's coiffure, and so on. And each time we rehearsed the desired movement, we'd go back to the *acting* of the scene with whatever improvements in the physical behavior were there. The fruits of this monitoring of the "inside" and the "outside" work in the scene session taught me, and the performers, the value of the *immediate* collaboration of the acting, voice, and movement instructions in approaching these matters of style.

Not only were scenes and monologues attacked in this

way, but a series of *études*, designed especially to prepare actors for nonnaturalistic performing, were executed under the joint supervision of the three instructors in the same sessions. We will soon be doing some of these exercises, using music and/or painting of various styles and periods as source material to create behavior from worlds distant from our present one. We will also learn songs and dances of all nations and all times. In this way, we'll approach the psychology and the behavior of peoples through the manifestations of their cultures as expressed by the artists of the time and place. And finally, work on choruses, with the voice/speech teacher and the movement teacher drilling the group and the acting teacher present, creates the possibility of getting a group of individuals *acting* in unison, if this is desired, rather than simply moving and intonating like abstract automatons.

Next, what can we look for in the rehearsal process that will ensure a normal growth of the "inside" and the "outside" together during the weeks from the first reading to the opening night and beyond?

Well, the worst thing you can do is to postpone matters of characterization until after you have settled your own inner sense of the truth of the scenes. It's too late then, baby. Nobody wants to disturb a fine sense of how *he* would behave, as rehearsed for days and days, with worries of how Mirabell in *The Way of the World* might walk and talk—to say nothing of his whole social outlook and milieu which, in fact, make up the essence of his character. If you try to "add" those considerations too late, you can only screw up that nice feeling of your own truth and lose what gains you've made in your rehearsal work so far. And if you say, "Oh, the hell with that superficial Restoration stuff that makes me feel so false now," you'll end up with yourself and Mrs. Millamant instead of Mirabell and Mrs. Millamant, and Congreve will "get you" from his grave.

I remember an admonition from my early training:

"Characterization is the overcoat you put on after you have all the under-dressing." Nonsense. What actually happens is that once you've got all that lovely underwear of thought and emotion going, you're so hot you never get around to the overcoat.

It's never too early, for example, to get all of the language problems out of the way. There's nothing more annoying than someone mispronouncing a name or word once, twice, three times in the early readings. After that, it becomes the devil's own job to get it straight. Next, find out what *every single word and phrase* meant in the time your play exists. In the breakdown I gave you of Act III, Scene ii in *Hamlet,* you'll discover that "sweet" means "dear," "just" is "well-balanced," "conversation" is "association," etc. Also, you'll appreciate the punning (a fine game at Wittenberg U., I'm sure) of Hamlet's "I will wear him in my heart's core"; "core," standing for "heart," gives him the idea to add, "ay, in my heart of heart." Etc. Etc.

Another bit of advice: scan early. ("But sóft! What líght through yónder wíndow bréaks?" is an example of a regular five-beat line.) You'll find some lines with the accent on the first, third, etc., syllables instead of on the second, fourth, etc. Also, some are mixed up. As you scan, you'll see how much pronunciation and meaning is revealed. And if you do it early, you can forget it early and allow the stresses to be scattered around a bit by the sense. But something of the respect for the inner rhythm of verse will have been established.

This next I only get by begging. *Enjoy* the sounds of the words and phrases. *Enjoy* the imagery. Learn to love your language. It is not your enemy—embrace it. And that goes not only for "beautiful" poetry, but all poetry: Beckett, Chekhov, Sam Shepard.

As you're facing up to the speech problems in your nonnaturalistic or noncontemporary part—no, better say *any* part requiring sound and movement far removed from your own daily patterns—you should also be solving any questions of the physical deportment of your character. First of all I always say, even at the first reading, "Sit into your part." In other words, if you are a King or a Queen, it's no use slouching in your chair and scratching the back of your head forever. You're only making the distance from where you are to where you have to go that much longer. If you are a Pope, uncross your legs. As soon as possible, get the feel of that robe draping to the floor. And the moment you're on your feet, simulate that robe with a substitute costume. If you're an early general in the field, work for that walk that distinguishes the horseman from the guy at the desk. And what happens to the voice used to giving orders to a thousand soldiers before they had those field telephones? Do improvisations of activities that go on in the normal course of your character's day—even if those exact activities don't turn up in the play.

Be brave about planning all your character elements— behavioral ideas, characteristic props, elements of costume, make-up, etc.—early on. All you have to be sure of is that, when you conceive these elements of characterization, you *justify* them with the proper inner choices in order to imbue them with truth. There's no point in deciding that your character "continuously looks behind him" unless the snap of your head backward derives from a deep-seated fear that someone may be following you. In this way, characterization, or "outside" work, acts as a guide to inner choices, just as inner choices find their expression in some sort of behavior. This approach keeps the idea of TOTAL acting operating and growing throughout the rehearsal period and creates an organic transformation of the actor into the character.

13

Style Exercises

Poetry is the greatest amount of emotion, with the greatest amount of order.

— Samuel Taylor Coleridge

EXERCISE:

I have here a pile of recordings, examples of music from every period and style: voodoo, Gregorian chants, Scarlatti sonatas, Charles Ives, punk rock, the lot. I want you to listen, with complete relaxation and full concentration, as I play the first choice. What will it suggest to you? If you get an idea, raise your hand. I will then play it through again as you improvise a scene based on your impressions derived from "drinking in" the music. It can be silent or otherwise. If it's a 78 record, I'll repeat it when it comes to the end, if you're not finished.

You are free to do something *to* the music, rhythmically, or *against* the music, or just to allow the music to serve as an emotionally suggestive background. Don't worry too much about "Mickey Mouse-ing" it, but rather be guided by whatever image the music conveys to you.

VARIATION:

This time, if anyone in the class feels that, while the improvisation is in progress, he or she can contribute to what is going on, get up and join in. Now you are guided both by the music and each other.

EXERCISE:

We have done some improvisations to music of all styles and periods. Now let's turn to painting. This exercise takes some time to prepare and complete. Pick a picture, by any artist in any time, from an art book, that has in it an interesting human figure in some fascinating, active pose. Study the painting carefully. You are not only going to reproduce it, you are going to bring it to life.

The first step is to assume the exact pose of the figure in the picture. But I mean *exact*, from the placement of every finger to the identical reproduction of the look on the face. From your study of the picture and the examination of your muscles in the pose, try to arrive at the *intention* of the subject. What is he doing at the moment the artist caught him? What is he thinking? In this way, you'll *justify* your pose. (Remember the "take a pose" exercise in our work on imagination?) Now give yourself some activity that would reproduce how this character would move about, sit down, etc. Remember to make all choices from within the intention you have chosen and are now extending. Also, and most importantly, the choices should be derived from the character in the painting, the style, the period, and so on. Use elements of cloth, or whatever you need, to simulate the costume and substitute props.

You now have made this static pose into a living character. Next, choose a text that this person might conceivably speak—either from a play or a poem, one that would go with your character and what you glean of his possible objectives. Break your text down as you would a scene. Wherever possible, use music to enhance the sense of period, create atmosphere, and so on. You have now developed a scene in which your sense of the style of your character is derived not only from his thinking but from the art of his period—the painting, the music, the poetry.

A talented actor in class once chose to use Manet's *The Dead Bullfighter.* I wondered how he was going to bring *this* painting to life. But he did, and most imaginatively, by inventing the following scenario: This bull fighter, after his elaborate dressing scene, went through a ceremony of prayers and invocations that included his fooling the angel of death by pretending to be dead *before* the bullfight. This whole number in the dressing room, with the intoning of Latin liturgical verses and the wild sound of the "Corrida de Toros" music coming from the bullring outside, made an unforgettable evocation of Manet's painting.

14

Acting in Opera and Musicals

> To achieve a harmony of music, singing, speech and
> action, one needs more than outer, physical tempo
> and rhythm; one needs inner, spiritual tempo and
> rhythm.
>
> —Constantin Stanislavsky

How can we use the elements of our acting craft in opera and
musicals? There's hardly anything we need discard, but
there are added conditions, and so some adaptation is called
for. The one great addition, of course, is the music itself. Now
we have *two* playwrights—the librettist and the composer.
In opera, the prime mover is the music, since it is fundamental and continuous; most musicals are more evenly weighted
between musical numbers and spoken dialogue.

Having worked in opera houses, I must say that too often
the only consideration of the singers (in addition to their
voices, of course) is the "blocking." I seldom heard anyone
ask, "*What* am I doing?" or, "*Why* am I doing it" (let alone,
"*How* am I doing it?"), but always, "*Where do I go?*" The
implication seems to be that if you sing well and hit your
right spot, the job is done. Once, after directing an opera, I
received a gracious thank-you note from the lovely prima
donna, saying, "I loved your blocking." There never was

enough rehearsal time to break the tradition of singers, having been coached by conductors (or their assistants) in the interpretation of the music, relying simply on the stage director for their movements. This system can be cracked sometimes and, when it is, it makes a hell of a difference in the acting. I was lucky when I directed Marc Blitzstein's *Regina* (based on Lillian Hellman's *The Little Foxes*) on Broadway because I had five uninterrupted weeks to work with the singers. Later, when I repeated my direction under opera house conditions at the old Fifty-fifth Street New York City Opera Company, most of the cast was retained and so had done the acting work already. Otherwise, it's tough. Margaret Webster, one of the first legitimate stage directors employed in an opera house, used to call the old Metropolitan Opera "Heartbreak House." I revised that, one day at the New York City Opera, to "Heartburn House" when a young singer, upon exiting a scene we were rehearsing, instead of waiting to get his corrections or do it over, kept going on down the hall to another rehearsal. I thought to myself that, in a play, I always make sure the character knows where he's coming from when he enters and where he's going when he exits. This guy was going into another show.

The closest many singers come to interpreting what they are singing is to "color" their tones in an attempt to clarify meaning. A quick, clear example is Maggie Teyte's recording of Martini's song "Plaisir d'Amour." She carefully colors the "plaisir" in "plaisir d'amour" and "chagrin" in the second phrase, "chagrin d'amour." There is real delight in the sound of "plaisir" and a sense of grief indicated in the "chagrin." Well and good—so far. But how can the singing actor, in addition to this kind of clear articulation, "talk" and "listen," as we understand the terms, with intention, and so play through the situation the character is in? He ought to be able to do this just as a good actor does, even though he is singing instead of talking. Then, truly, operas would be music dramas, or "sung plays." Anyone lucky enough to have seen the best of Walter Felsenstein's productions at the East Berlin Komische Oper will know what I mean. There was a complete sense of ensemble playing, just as one would expect from a fine theatre troupe. The only difference was—they were singing. (And they took up to six months to rehearse a production.)

The main stumbling block is how to get the thinking (intention) going, not only through the words now, but through the music as well. If poetic language tends to make speaking actors who are not "talking" properly sound affected, you can imagine how music affects the singing actor. It results in that sound of self-indulgent, generalized "expression" that we all recognize so well, even when the opera is sung in English.

Here's a suggestion: First, go through the scene without the music. (Franco Corelli told me that, in the early days when he sang with Maria Callas in Europe, she always made him read through the scenes with her, without the piano, before they got to singing. So you see I'm in good company.) Do all the work a speaking actor would do in his early rehearsals—good "talking" and "listening" read-throughs, making general choices gleaned from the production talk (if one is not forthcoming from the stage director, do your own), including the overall objective of your role, character elements, and so forth, and then breaking down the sections of the scene into your intentions gleaned from suggestions in the text *and* a careful examination of the music.

In musicals, your objectives probably will be suggested mainly by the dialogue and the lyrics of the musical sections. But if the score is written by a good composer of dramatic music (and not a song writer of interpolated numbers), you will certainly be helped to zero in on specific intentions suggested by the music.

In opera, on the other hand, where the better of the two

dramatists (composer and librettist) might be the musician—
Verdi, for example—you will often find stronger clues as to
what the subtext is by a careful examination of the musical
material, either in the vocal line or the orchestration, or both.
The change in tempo and the held B♭ with the fall into the
G, that begins "*Dite alla giovine*" in the second act of
Traviata, describe ever so much more dramatically than the
text alone does, Violetta's intention to capitulate to Alfredo's
father's request for her to give his son up.

When you are playing your situation as fully as you can
(still in the chairs), call in the pianist. Now read through the
scene, still talking, as the pianist plays the music, trying to fit
your speaking to the space provided by the music, all the
time keeping the same intentions going. You'll find, of
course, that as you talk, the spacing is different. For example:
where, before, you could answer her on cue, you now have
four bars of music to wait before you speak that must be filled
with something other than clearing your throat and preparing "la voce" for the next assault. Your choices are many. In
those four bars you could be (1) continuing the thought you
had when you were listening to your partner and then starting your next objective when you pick up your cue, or (2)
starting your next intention as she finishes her phrase and
merely holding off expressing it for four bars—for a justifiable
reason, of course (viz. to let her swing slowly in the wind for
a moment), or (3) having an action that is different both from
what you were thinking while listening and what you will do
when coming in on your cue, and so on. In this way, you are
"spacing" your inner line to fit the pattern of the music, and
you don't always have to worry about filling up those four
bars with useless "business" or a cross that's equally pointless.

You are finally ready to go through the scene again, this
time singing. What will happen now can only *enhance* your
objectives, as singing, an extension of talking, will serve to
warm up your inner line with feeling. Without following this

procedure, you might have all mood and no inner action. A continuous inner line is what will prevent all that starting and stopping, standing around and lurching, that is the plague of so much opera acting.

When we come to musicals, additional problems present themselves. How can the actors help to avoid the dynamic breaks that occur at the beginnings and ends of musical numbers? Sometimes, of course, you may want the shock of attack as a number starts. More often, some sort of blend is needed as you pass from speech to song and back again. I have often observed the coughing and restlessness in the audience that accompanies the resumption of "lifelike" dialogue after the smash finish of a musical number. Devices such as a bit of reprise music, slowly fading away under the ensuing dialogue, are just that—devices.

I remember that Agnes deMille (the choreographer with whom I did several shows, starting with *Brigadoon*) tried, wherever possible, to blend her movement from walking to dancing and so eliminate the "seams." So, too, I would ask the singing actors to intensify their speaking, with some chosen justification always, as they got right up to their singing cue. Also, where feasible, I had them half-talk the opening words of the song. In this way you can completely obliterate any break in the dynamic line as you go from the dialogue scene into the musical portion. Then, at the end of the number, I always found a way to attack the beginning of the speaking part with a significance that grabbed the audience's attention and allowed for no letdown from the number. Gradually, the normal dynamics of dialogue were resumed. In this way, singers (and dancers) cooperate in solving one of the director's special problems of the form of musical theatre.

To sum up, the acting principles outlined so far to give form (and substance) to "straight" plays should prevail. Of course, each medium brings with it its own special demands

—whether it be film, television, opera, or whatever. Basically, though, for the singing actor in musicals or opera, the idea of making the "inside" (intention) and the "outside" (voice and movement) operate together, indeed, derive from each other, is devoutly to be wished.

15

L'Envoi

Time, place and action may with pains be wrought,
but genius must be born, and never can be taught.

—John Dryden

Suppose you did all the exercises in this course. Suppose you understood all the points made in the explanations and the notes. Would that make you a good actor? Maybe, maybe not. Why not? Well, for the simple reason that we haven't taken into account that little thing called talent. And although a clever eye can detect whether or not it is present, it is almost impossible to define.

If we say sensitivity is one of the ingredients of a talented actor, what about the sensitive people you know who just aren't good actors? If imagination is required, and it is, we can point to extremely imaginative people who are not successful playing on the stage. What of those folks, so highly emotional that they cry at the stage directions, but who can't put their feelings to any practical use in the theatre? And so on, down through all the elements of the craft.

All right, then, what *does* distinguish the imaginative, sensitive, emotional person, who has studied the acting craft thoroughly and intelligently, from the talented actor? It can't just be the so-called performer's ego. I've known some fine actors who were terribly shy, even self-effacing. Certainly, you have to have the ability to be proficient in all the elements of the actor's craft and to be able, on stage, to use them to interpret parts. But even *that's* not enough.

You must have that unconscious gift of being able, while creating on stage, to grab the audience in a way that makes them watch what you are doing and care about what you are doing. This indefinable gift is what no one can teach. I have stood on stage with actors, knowing they were really living through their situation truthfully and seeming to find the expressive means to dramatize that truthful experience. Yet it would turn out the audience couldn't have cared less. It was as if, somewhere between the stage and the auditorium, an invisible curtain existed that sifted and diluted those actors' creative powers. But I have also sat in theatres where I could actually feel waves of welcome greet the efforts of certain other performers. Personality, you say? I don't know. I only know that if you don't have it, no one can help you get it. Sorry.

For consolation, I'll leave you with one of my favorite quotes on the subject of acting. It is called "Demands of the Actor, in Ancient India":

> Freshness, beauty, a pleasant broad face, red lips, beautiful teeth, a neck round as a bracelet, beautifully formed hands, graceful build, powerful hips, charm, grace, dignity, nobility, pride, not to speak of the quality of talent.